D1526844

Cosmopolitanism and Solidarity

❖ STUDIES IN AMERICAN THOUGHT ❖
AND CULTURE

Series Editor

Paul S. Boyer

Cosmopolitanism and Solidarity

Studies in Ethnoracial, Religious, and Professional Affiliation in the United States

David A. Hollinger

THE UNIVERSITY OF WISCONSIN PRESS

The University of Wisconsin Press
1930 Monroe Street
Madison, Wisconsin 53711

www.wisc.edu/wisconsinpress/

3 Henrietta Street
London WC2E 8LU, England

1   3   5   4   2

Printed in the United States of America

Library of Congress Cataloging-in-Publication Data
Hollinger, David A.
Cosmopolitanism and solidarity : studies in ethnoracial, religious, and
professional affiliation in the United States / David A. Hollinger.
p.   cm.—(Studies in American thought and culture)
Includes bibliographical references and index.
ISBN-13: 978-0-299-21660-3 (hard cover: alk. paper)
1. Multiculturalism—United States.   2. Cosmopolitanism—United States.
3. Solidarity—United States.   4. Cultural relativism—United States.
5. United States—Race relations.   6. United States—Ethnic relations.
7. United States—Religion.   8. Education, Higher—Social aspects—
United States.   9. Church and education—United States.
10. Christianity and culture—United States.
I. Title.   II. Series.
E184.A1H636   2006
305.800973—dc22   2005032876

**This book was published with the support of
the Anonymous Fund for the Humanities
of the University of Wisconsin–Madison.**

For two very lively Hollingers born a century apart

My Aunt
Annie A. Hollinger
born 1905

and

My Grandson
Aidan David Hollinger-Miles
born 2005

Contents

Preface

Just who belongs together with whom, and for what purposes, and on what authority? The answers to these basic issues in affiliation are not as obvious as they once seemed. Ascribed and taken-for-granted identities are being disrupted by a multitude of social transformations throughout the world, especially in the United States. The problem of solidarity is emerging as one of the central challenges of the twenty-first century. The analytic essays and critical interventions of 2000–2005 collected in this volume are united by my engagement with this problem and with cosmopolitan responses to it.

What do I mean by "the problem of solidarity"? How does "cosmopolitanism" respond to it? Why is the history of United States a potentially helpful resource for anyone interested in the global problem of solidarity? By speaking to these three questions in this preface, I hope to clarify the concerns that drive the writings collected here. But before I turn to these questions, I want briefly to describe the character of these pieces, explain the circumstances of their composition, and thank several people and institutions to whom I am indebted.

Several of these pieces focus on communities of descent—my preferred term for what are often called "races" or "ethnic groups"—and the processes by which the borders of these communities are maintained or altered. Some of the other pieces address religious, civic, and professional associations. Each was designed for a particular occasion or with a highly specific analytic task in mind, so it will not do to exaggerate the thematic unity of this collection. Yet I have written a headnote for each, calling attention to connections between them and sometimes expressing second thoughts. All nine appear in these pages unchanged from the text of their original publication in scattered journals and books, with the exception of a few small errors of fact I have taken this opportunity to correct. *Cosmopolitanism and Solidarity* builds directly upon my two previous books. *Postethnic America: Beyond Multiculturalism* (New York, 1995; third expanded edition, 2006) focused on the problem of solidarity as displayed in the debates over multiculturalism in the United States. *Science, Jews, and Secular Culture: Studies in Mid-Twentieth Century American Intellectual History* (Princeton, 1996) explored the writings and careers of two generations of American intellectuals especially attracted to cosmopolitanism.

Some of what now appears in *Cosmopolitanism and Solidarity* was first drafted for presentation as the Merle Curti Lectures under this title at the University of Wisconsin at Madison in 2000. Hence it is appropriate that this volume be published by the University of Wisconsin Press. I thank the Department of History of that campus for the honor of serving as Merle Curti Lecturer. I also thank the Institute for Advanced Study in Princeton, New Jersey, and Queens College of the University of Oxford, two hospitable locations where I completed some of the essays collected here. Most of all I thank my wonderful academic home, the University of California at Berkeley, filled with faculty colleagues, students, and staff who sustain me on a daily basis. I also owe much to collegial conversations with individuals acknowledged in the journals and books where these pieces were originally published. But here I want to mention the several people in Berkeley to whom I feel the most deeply indebted: Carol J. Clover, Carla Hesse, Joan Heifetz Hollinger, Martin Jay, Thomas W. Laqueur, John Lie, and Yuri Slezkine. Beyond Berkeley, my greatest debts are to James T. Kloppenberg and Werner Sollors of Harvard

University. For carrying *Cosmopolitanism and Solidarity* through the publication process, I am grateful to Paul S. Boyer.

So, what *do* I mean by "the problem of solidarity"?

Solidarity is an experience of willed affiliation. Some might prefer to speak of "the problem of community," but this usage blurs more than it clarifies. Solidarity entails a greater degree of conscious commitment, even if that commitment is inspired by inherited expectations. The word *solidarity* best serves us if we use it to denote a state of social existence more specific than what the word *community* has come to mean. The latter often serves simply to classify people, to denote a group defined by one or more characteristics shared by its members whether or not those members are disposed to act together. Hence we speak of "the real estate community," "the gay community," "the Asian American community," "the scientific community," "the national community," "the upper west side community," "the manufacturing community," "the golfing community," and so on, indicating what may be an organized interest group or may be nothing more than a collectivity of individuals who share a distinguishing trait or practice or place of residence. Solidarity is a state of social existence achieved only when parties to an affiliation are understood to exercise at least *some* measure of agency, if only in consciously affirming an affiliation into which they were born. The experience of solidarity is more active than mere membership in a community. When the word *solidarity* entered the English language in the middle of the nineteenth century, it was understood to refer to a property that some communities possessed and others did not. The English word *community*, understood to denote a body of individuals, dates back many more centuries. Solidarity is more performative than is community. It implies, even in modest dimensions, a special claim that individuals have on each other's energies and compassion.

What is at semantic issue can be illuminated when we consider the popular notion of a "community of fate." This term commonly refers to a collectivity whose members have been subject to a single set of historical constraints. Jews are often described as a community of fate. Many Jews also affiliate with one another, affirm Jewish identity, and help to constitute a vigorous and sustaining solidarity. But not all members of the Jewish community of fate demonstrate significant solidarity with other Jews. The same distinction can apply to black people in the United States, to other descent-defined groups, to women, and to any population group whose members have been treated in some special fashion by persons who have exercised power over them. A community of fate will often sustain a solidarity, but the problem of solidarity arises only when the role of "fate" is complicated by the action of forces other than those that created a given "community of fate" to begin with. Feminism is a solidarity, but womanhood is not. Judaism is a solidarity but having a Jewish ancestor—even a Jewish mother, to allude to one of the classic criteria for being counted as a Jew—is not. The Chinese American community is a solidarity for many Americans of Chinese ancestry, but not every American of Chinese ancestry is equally invested in it and some may be altogether indifferent to it. We will miss the character and scope of the problem of solidarity in the twenty-first century if we conflate solidarity with the mere possession of a set of traits or antecedents or confinements. The problem of solidarity is real when there is at least some opportunity for choice, when people can exercise some influence over just what "we" they help to constitute.

The problem of solidarity is thus at hand whenever people are capable of actually asking, who are "we"? This "we question" is not new, but it now arises with some urgency in an imposing range of settings throughout the world. The question does not press itself upon individuals who are supremely confident about the groups to which they belong, and to which they are the most deeply committed. Such people know their basic "identity," even if only because they have been told repeatedly what it is. They may never have had cause to question it, and may never have been allowed any choice in the matter. Uncontested ascription has always been a powerful adhesive, and often still is. But for millions in many parts of the globe today, this confidence has been challenged by a multitude of events, some of which are world-historical in scope.

Prominent among the events that enable us to recognize the shape of the problem of solidarity is the accelerating integration of the global capitalist economy and its attendant communications systems. New affiliations are created, while old ones are dissolved. "All that is solid melts into air," Karl Marx and Friedrich Engels observed even of the capitalism of their era. Capitalism has its own sources of stability, but capitalism has little respect for any affiliations that cannot be turned to its own purposes. Demographic migration, often attendant upon the dynamics of the world capitalist economy, is another major phenomenon threatening inherited associations. The movement of masses of people is nothing new, but now we see it in huge proportions, creating diasporas in the older industrial centers of Europe and North America, and creating sprawling mega-cities like Lagos and Sao Paolo, which our demographers tell us will be the chief social settings of population growth in the next half century. This physical mobility affects both migrants and the peoples into whose company they move: the migrants and their offspring can be divided between diasporic consciousness and new national or regional identities, while groups with a proprietary relation to a land and its institutions—such as the British and the Dutch and many other classically European peoples now coming to grips with the reality of immigration—wonder if the newcomers alter the character of their "we."

As the example of Europeans uncertain about immigration can illustrate, staying at home is not necessarily an escape from the problem of solidarity. Other disruptive events can come to you, even if you do not stir. Regime-changes and the decline of empires, as well as immigration, can prompt the "we question" for people who stay put. A host of post-Soviet states in Central Asia and Eastern Europe affirm their own peoplehood against the Soviet identity of the recent past. Ethnic Russians in the Baltic states and elsewhere in once-Soviet lands find themselves outsiders. In Africa and Asia an even larger number of post-imperial nations negotiate their state authority with a diversity of descent communities whose relations to one another were heavily structured by the European conquerors who drew the boundaries of the states now trying to maintain themselves. Meanwhile, in the uniquely conspicuous space of Western Europe, affiliation as "European" now rivals Dutch, German, Italian, and other national identities more often than at any time since the rise of the nation state as the basic unit of political organization.

In the realm of learned discourse countless intellectuals explain ever and ever more earnestly that all population groups, even those once called "races," are historically contingent constructions. This truth is especially hard to evade in the United States, where marriage, cohabitation, and reproduction across "racial" lines have increased rapidly. The invidious process of "racializing" the varieties of non-white Americans continues, yet never in the history of the Republic has this process been more energetically contested and never has the very concept of race been more persistently attacked. But well beyond the United States the fact of physical as well as cultural mixing confounds ascribed identities. This mixing prompts the "we" question and leads many individuals, especially in democratic countries, to think—no doubt naively in many cases—that they can answer this question for themselves.

The point of alluding to recent events is not to insist that the challenge these events generate is altogether unprecedented. Historians more confident than I of their own knowledge of the entire past of our species can quarrel about the uniqueness of our time if they wish. My claim here is more modest: these recent events, the consequences of which contemporary thinkers are only beginning to assess, make it plausible to suppose that among the great problems of the twenty-first century is the problem of willed affiliation, the problem of solidarity.

I suggest this without doubting for an instant the enduring value for the twenty-first century of W. E. B. Du Bois's classic formulation for the twentieth. "The problem of the Twentieth Century," said Du Bois in 1903, "is the problem of the color-line." But the lines between colors are not as sharp today as they were a century ago, or even fifty years ago, and the significance of color itself is more vigorously contested, thanks in large part to twentieth-century men and women whose actions vindicated Du Bois's prophecy. The more that we come to see the color-coded "races" as artifacts, as contingent results of human action rather than primordial causes of it, the more does the color line take its place among other social distinctions that may or may not be the basis for the assigning or choosing of affiliations. To be sure, poetic license is implicit in any assertion that any single problem defines a century. I invoke and emulate Du Bois's prescient hyperbole only to convey what I take to be the range and depth of the problem of solidarity.

If Du Bois were with us today, he would probably be among the first to warn that it is easy to exaggerate the degree of choice opened up by the world-historical transformations to which I have alluded. The problem of solidarity is inevitably located within one or another set of historical constraints, including the way in which power is distributed in any particular social setting. Some people have much more authority over their own affiliations than others do. The scholars who have reminded us of the decidedly artifactual status of even the population groups long considered primordial have also understood, for the most part, that artifacts can be deeply entrenched. Contingency does not imply easy rearrangement. Yet solidarity is worth talking about as a "problem" rather than simply as a condition only when the sources of social cohesion are not absolutely fixed.

And when they are not fixed, a tension often appears that gives social-psychological structure to the problem of solidarity. The tension is between the needs for 1) a deep feeling of social belonging, enabling intimacy and promoting mutual exchange, and 2) a broad alliance, enabling mutual defense and facilitating a greater range of social and cultural experience. Solidarities narrow enough to serve the need for belonging threaten to close people off from a larger world of realities some of which may damage them if not engaged. Solidarities broad enough to be consistently engaged with this larger world threaten to become too broad to sustain a sense of belonging. This tension between the impulse for concentration and the impulse for incorporation is heightened as economic and communications systems allow ostensibly distant forces to impinge on one's "home." Global warming is a convenient example of a threat to everyone that is difficult to engage from the point of view of any solidarity smaller that the species. But any solidarity capacious enough to act effectively on problems located in a large arena is poorly suited to satisfy the human need for belonging. And any solidarity tight enough to serve the need for belonging cannot be expected to respond effectively to challenges common to a larger and more heterogeneous population. To be sure, one can have multiple affiliations, many "we's," some more capacious than others, but the energies and resources and affections of individuals are not infinite in supply. There are priorities to be set.

Hence the problem of solidarity has a political-economic structure as well as a social-psychological one. We can speak of a "political economy of solidarity" because solidarity is a commodity distributed by authority. At issue is the distribution of affections, resources, and energies. Whether identity is understood as monolithic or multiple, enduring or contingent, it has a political economy: the political economy of solidarity. On just whose affections, resources, and energies can one make a special claim, and who has a special claim on one's own supply? And what authority decides? Central to the history of nationalism, after all, has been the use of state power to establish certain "identities," understood as performative, and thus creating social cohesion on certain terms rather than others. The "identity debates" of the United States of recent decades have been largely driven by this concern to distribute the energies that make solidarities. The United States is filled with people eager to tell other people what their identity is— where they really "belong"—although the practice is common wherever identity is understood as performative. Quarrels about "mixed race" people are a prominent example of the operation of the political economy of solidarity, as a variety of interest groups offer claims and counter claims about the identity of these individuals. A flashpoint for these disputes in the United States is the federal census, on which individuals are expected to identify themselves according to color-coded population groups. In the case of the federal census, then, the de facto authority is physical characteristics, especially skin pigmentation and facial shape, but the de jure authority is the will of the individual being classified.

Where does "cosmopolitanism" come in? Cosmopolitanism is, among other things, a family of responses to the problem of solidarity. Cosmopolitanism promotes broadly based, internally complex, multiple solidarities equipped to confront the large-scale dilemmas of a "globalizing" epoch while attending to the endemic human need for intimate belonging. Cosmopolitanism seeks to maximize the authority of individual wills and to minimize that of ascribed identities. But cosmopolitanism has its own semantic difficulties. By confronting those difficulties here, we can best distinguish it from other approaches to the problem of solidarity.

Cosmopolitanism is often associated with the Enlightenment of eighteenth-century Konigsberg and Paris, and consequently has been suspected of being too abstract and too absolute to offer much help in our own times. People calling themselves cosmopolitans are frequently on the defensive, accused of being insufficiently responsive to diversity, particularity, history, the masses of humankind, the realities of power, and the need for politically viable solidarities. Hence we have seen in recent years a proliferation of adjectives invoked to neutralize these suspicions. We have "rooted cosmopolitanism," calculated to counter the older, "rootless cosmopolitanism" so often mocked as irrelevant to earthly affairs if not subversive of sound loyalties. We also encounter cosmopolitanisms described as "discrepant," "critical," "situated," "patriotic," and "realistic." The point of these modifiers is not to distinguish different contemporary schools of cosmopolitan thought from one another, as it might first appear, but to define them against a cosmopolitanism of the past that is now perceived as unable to deliver vital goods that nationalists, provincials, parochials, tribalists, and other proudly down-to-earth persuasions claim to retail. What these modifiers most try to do is to distinguish cosmopolitanism from universalism. Indeed, the two concepts have a long history together. But now it makes good sense to use the words *cosmopolitanism* and *universalism* to denote rather different dispositions.

We can, as I have argued in *Postethnic America* and elsewhere, distinguish between a universalist will to find common ground and a cosmopolitan will to engage human diversity. For cosmopolitans, the diversity of humankind is fact and something of an opportunity; for universalists it is a challenge. Cosmopolitanism shares with universalism a suspicion of enclosures, but the cosmopolitan understands the necessity of enclosures in their capacity as contingent and provisionally bounded domains in which people can form intimate and sustaining relationships, can create diversity, and can protect threatened constituencies against outside forces. Cosmopolitanism urges each individual and collective unit to absorb as much varied experience as it can while retaining its capacity to achieve self-definition and to advance its own aims effectively. Cosmopolitanism differs from universalism in the respect it shows for the instincts to give special treatment to those with whom one is most intimately connected and by whom one is socially sustained. Cosmopolitanism respects the honest difficulties than even the most humane and generous people have in achieving solidarity with persons they perceive as very different from themselves. Cosmopolitans are reserved toward the inspiring, universalist aphorism of Rabindranath Tagore to the effect that "the Gods of humanity shall appear in the ruins of the temple of the tribe." The claims of tribes and nations are not always products of hate. These claims are sometimes advanced as instrumental reactions to the inequities of the world capitalist economy and the cultural hegemony of the North Atlantic West.

Yet cosmopolitanism's acceptance of diversity and of bounded social units is not to be conflated with another set of diversity-affirming, group-appreciating projects that often arise within nation-states like the United States, Canada, and India whose population includes a number of distinctive communities of descent and religious communities. We can best call this other cluster of approaches by the name of *pluralism*. Pluralists emphasize the boundaries between groups, and often ask for group rights and other special, constitutional and cultural privileges. Cosmopolitanism and pluralism have often been allied in the common cause of promoting tolerance, and in efforts to recognize and celebrate diversity. In some contexts, they are taken to be the same thing. But cosmopolitanism is more liberal in style; it is more oriented to the individual, and supposes that individuals will be simultaneously affiliated with a number of groups, including civic and religious communities, as well as communities of descent. Pluralism is more conservative in style; it is oriented to the preexisting group, and it is likely to ascribe to each individual a primary identity within a single community of descent. Pluralists are more concerned to protect and perpetuate the cultures of groups already well established at the time the ideal of pluralism is invoked, while cosmopolitans are more inclined to encourage the voluntary formation of new communities of wider scope made possible by altered historical circumstances and demographic mixing. Cosmopolitans are specialists in the creating of the new, while cautious about destroying the old; pluralists are specialists in the conservation of the old, while cautious about the new. Both are more sensitive than universalists generally are to the need for sustaining solidarities smaller than the species, but they differ in the value they assign to inherited boundaries, and in the value they assign to the consent of individuals to the affiliations that bind them.

What I have just characterized as "cosmopolitanism" is the disposition I elaborated and defended in *Postethnic America*, especially when advancing the principle of "affiliation by revocable consent" as a counter to the ascribed identities often preferred by my interlocutors within the debates of the 1990s over multiculturalism. Here I will not go over more of the ground covered in that book, but I allude to it by way of underscoring the sense of cosmopolitanism assumed by the writings collected in *Cosmopolitanism and Solidarity*. This cosmopolitanism is directed the most obviously against the blood-and-soil, racializing versions of nationalism promoted by the classical European nation states. Basic to this nationalism is the phenomenon my colleague John Lie has recently called "modern peoplehood." This is, Lie explains,

> an inclusionary and involuntary group identity with a putatively shared history and distinct way of life. It is inclusionary because everyone in the group, regardless of status, gender, or moral worth, belongs. It is involuntary because one is born into an ascriptive category of peoplehood. In addition to common descent—a shared sense of genealogy and geography—contemporary commonality, such as language, religion, culture, or consciousness, characterizes the group.

But cosmopolitanism is also a rival to, and in some contexts a collegial successor to another set of responses to the problem of solidarity: the counter-racist movements that have reproduced the racializing practices of "modern peoplehood"—often in the name of "multiculturalism"—even while in revolt against the nation states that exemplified it. These counter-racist movements within and beyond the United States are extreme extensions of the "pluralism" I described above. Lie reminds us that these counter-racist practices often "use the oppressor's language, ideals, and methods," and in so doing are themselves confined by the increasingly anachronistic practice of "modern peoplehood." One might so construe the early writings of Du Bois himself, when, inspired by his study of German philosophy and literature, he exalted the distinctive genius of each race. Franz Fanon understood this when he described "Black soul" as "but a white artifact." Cosmopolitans appreciate the historical particularity of circumstances in which these strategic uses of racialization have emerged. In some situations, a descent-defined solidarity has proved to be the only viable mode of social cohesion with any hope of offering mutual support and political defense. Indeed, one of the chief points of difference between cosmopolitans and universalists is that cosmopolitans are more likely to understand that the answers they might prescribe to the problem of solidarity in the United States or Western Europe are not suitable for everyone in every situation.

But the increasing popularity of cosmopolitanism in recent years reflects the feeling that the world-historical events I invoked earlier in this preface have diminished the spaces in which the old, racialist forms of anti-racism can do much good. This is not the place to attempt an overview of the countless books, articles, manifestos, and position papers that have made cosmopolitanism one of the prominent political and cultural movements of the turn of the twenty-first century. Nor is this the place to acknowledge the differences between leading voices in this movement. Yet I do want to list the names of the some of the most engaged and effective of the voices known to me: Alexander Aleinikoff, Kwame Anthony Appiah, Roger Baubock, Ulrich Beck, Thomas Bender, Seyla Benhabib, Rogers Brubaker, Craig Calhoun, Pheng Cheah,

Amos Elon, Paul Gilroy, Amy Gutmann, David Held, Jennifer Hochschild, Michael Ignatieff, Mary Kaldor, Bruno Latour, John Lie, Bharati Mukherjee, Bhikhu Parekh, Ross Posnock, Bruce Robbins, Salman Rushdie, Samuel Scheffler, Rogers Smith, Amartya Sen, Werner Sollors, and Jeremy Waldron.

Some of these have developed extensive programs for global governance and cultural liberation, the virtues and deficiencies of which are far beyond the scope of my summary remarks here. I simply want to convey the core of cosmopolitanism, considered as an extended family of responses to the problem of solidarity, and to point to one supremely important insight about our contemporary world that I believe is understood by everyone I just named: *if you do not take on as much of the world as you can, the world will come to you, and on terms over which you will have even less control than you did previously.* There are fewer and fewer places to hide from forces that operate in a global arena. "There's no hiding place down there," warned an old gospel song. Nor is there a hiding place "up here." Wide solidarities are demanded by our historical situation. Cosmopolitanism, whatever its limitations, truly understands this.

W̲hy is the history of the United States of special interest in this context of an attraction to cosmopolitan responses to the problem of solidarity? The United States has been a major site for many of the processes that now produce the problem of solidarity elsewhere. The United States has also been a testing ground for many different responses to these processes. The United States is not so much a model for the world as an archive of experience on which the world can draw critically.

The more contingent become the groups to which individuals throughout the world belong, the more relevant the history of the United States appears to be. The United States is not the only nation-state to be demographically derived from multiple immigrations, but it is a highly conspicuous case. The United States is not the only nation-state to be ideologically committed to the autonomy of the individual citizen, but here, too, it is a highly conspicuous case. The United States is not the only nation-state to be subject to the demands of an aggressive capitalism, but to say that the United States is conspicuous in this respect is surely a crashing understatement. These three classical sources of contingency—of a life always shifting and producing new connections between individuals—do not exhaust the life story of this exceptionally dynamic society. Yet the United States is a prodigious example of all three. These familiar features of the United States may or may not justify an "American exceptionalist" interpretation of modern history, but surely these features are vital enough to recommend this history of the United States to the close attention of anyone interested in the problem of solidarity, and render surprising the slowness of the academic establishments of many other nations to devote more energy to the study of this history.

But the list of relevant aspects of the history of the United States is easily extended. The United States carries a legacy of race-specific chattel slavery, and thus confronts its Enlightenment-derived egalitarian principles with one of the most deeply embedded racisms to be found anywhere in the modern world. The United States has become the home to the largest Jewish population in the history of the Disapora, making it a site for the flourishing of the single demographic group that has proved to the most responsive to the global modernization processes entailing science, capitalism, socialism, and modernist movements in the arts. The United States has alternately exterminated and incorporated peoples it has conquered militarily, and thus represents both extremes of dealing with alterity. The United States has been the scene of the physical and cultural mixing of descent groups from all continents, and presents to the world a more ethnoracially diverse face than does Argentina, China, Egypt, France, Germany, India, Iran, Italy, Japan, Nigeria, Russia, Thailand, Turkey, Ukraine, or the United Kingdom. The United States has actually defined itself as an immigrant-receiving nation, something that many other immigrant-receiving nations, especially in Europe, have not done, even today. The population of the United States is the most religiously affirming of any industrialized nation despite a strong tradition of church-state separation, bearing witness to the appeal of voluntary associations independent of state power. Intellectually, the United States is the matrix for many of the most extensively developed and empirically warranted arguments that standardized population groups are artifacts rather than natural kinds. The national project of the United States is the most successful in all of modern history, as measured by duration and power: it is the only major nation state in the twenty-first century to operate under a constitution written in the eighteenth. The nationalism of the United States is officially civic rather than ethnic in its principles—however frequently its governments and its citizens have violated those principles—and thus is sharply at odds with the more ethnic nationalisms of classic European model. Yet for all its connections to the world, its electorate is one of the most insular in the industrialized North Atlantic West: the American government's persistent refusal to appreciate the perspectives of other nations has become more rigid since the end of the Cold War, and exemplifies the cloistering, parochializing effect that a preponderance of military and economic power can have even on a "global" nation. It has become more an empire than ever before despite a vigorously anti-imperialist ideological tradition, and, like so many empires, it is led by people whose sense of "we" is extremely narrow. Hence the United States is far from serving as a sterling examplar of cosmopolitanism; rather, it is a site, like many other nations, for struggles over the problem of solidarity in which cosmopolitanism is an active but not a dominant player.

A handful of these struggles within the United States are the chief topics of the writings collected in *Cosmopolitanism and Solidarity*. In this preface I have sketched the rudimentary outlook on American history in global perspective that has informed *Postethnic America* and *Science, Jews, and Secular Culture* as well as the writings collected here, but *Cosmopolitanism and Solidarity* does not pretend to address more than a few of the recent historical episodes that inspire scrutiny in relation to the problem of solidarity. Each piece was written to stand on its own, and will be of interest, I hope, even to readers who do not share my own sense of the centrality to our time of the problem of solidarity.

Berkeley, California
February 2005

Cosmopolitanism and Solidarity

1

Amalgamation and Hypodescent

The Question of Ethnoracial Mixture in
the History of the United States

*This essay argues that marriage and reproduction across the lines divid-
ing the standardized, population groups is a much greater reality in
the history of the United States than even the popular discourse about "the
melting pot" has recognized. Confronting the truth about descent mixture is important because that truth helps us to understand the actual dynamics of racialization, and to thereby recognize the historically contingent character of the
categories that we call racial and ethnic groups. The more we recognize the
contingency of group boundaries, and above all the role of government power
in creating and sustaining these boundaries, the sounder the perspective we can
achieve on the relationship between the national solidarity of the United States
and the various subnational and transnational solidarities defined by common
descent. Part of that sounder perspective, I argue, is that not all ethnoracial minorities have experienced the same relationship with the empowered European
American majority. An accurate view of the combined histories of a) miscegenation law and b) the practice of classifying as black any person with any
visible trace of African ancestry reminds us that only black people inherit a
multi-century legacy of color-specific enslavement and institutionalized debasement under the constitutional authority of the United States.*

3

Some readers have worried that I am inadvertently reinforcing the anachronistic concept of "race" when I accept as analytic categories the entities we popularly call races (e.g., "African Americans"). But the implication of my analysis is instead to render the traditional notion of race all the more anachronistic. A few have assumed the essay is simply another in the long series of works fascinated by the dynamics of "interracial sex," but my clear concern is rather with the formation of families and the genetic mixing that follow from sex between members of different descent groups. Although I explicitly warn against the fantasy that interracial sex is the country's salvation, some readers have found it easier to accuse me of sharing in that fantasy than to join in the honest exploration of just what the prevalence of long-denied descent mixture means for the United States. A few readers have taken this essay to underestimate the power of racism in American society, but on the contrary the point is to more precisely locate and measure that racism in order to promote more direct and effective engagements with its dreadful effects.

After publishing this essay I was asked to spell out the relationship I posit here between the "one drop rule" for deciding which Americans are black and the "one hate rule" for deciding which Americans are to be the beneficiaries of anti-discrimination remedies. Hence I wrote the essay that I reprint immediately following this one, which is a more policy-engaged sequel to "Amalgamation and Hypodescent."

This article first appeared in American Historical Review *108 (2003): 1363–90.*

In the middle of a July night in 1958, a couple living in a small town in Virginia were awakened when a party of local police officers walked into their bedroom and arrested them for a felony violation of Virginia's miscegenation statute. The couple had been married in the District of Columbia, which did allow blacks and whites to marry each other, but the two Virginians were subsequently found guilty of violating the statute's prohibition on marrying out of state with the intent of circumventing Virginia law.[1]

That same summer, Hannah Arendt, the distinguished political theorist, an émigré from Hitler's Germany then living in New

York City, was writing an essay on school integration. That issue had been brought to flashpoint the previous year in Little Rock, Arkansas, by President Eisenhower's use of federal troops to enforce the ruling of the U.S. Supreme Court that public schools were no longer to be racially segregated. But Arendt used her essay on school integration, which had been commissioned by the editors of *Commentary,* to talk also about miscegenation laws. Arendt seems not to have known of what was happening in Virginia that summer to Richard and Mildred Loving, the couple whose last name was such a fitting emblem for a relationship that was being denied the sanction of law. But Arendt insisted that, whatever the injustice entailed by the segregation of public schools, a deeper injustice by far was any restriction on an individual's choice of a spouse. The laws that make "mixed marriage a criminal offense," Arendt declared, were "the most outrageous" of the racist regulations then in effect in the American South.[2]

The stunned editors of *Commentary* balked. An aghast Sidney Hook, to whom the editors showed a copy, rushed into print in another magazine to complain that Arendt was making "equality in the bedroom" seem more important than "equality in education."[3] Arendt's essay daring to suggest that the civil rights movement had gotten its priorities wrong later appeared in yet another magazine, the more radical *Dissent*, but only as prefaced by a strong editorial disclaimer and then followed by two rebuttals, one of which actually defended legal restrictions on interracial marriage. A well-meaning European refugee, said by friends to be hopelessly naïve about the United States, had raised publicly the very last topic that advocates of civil rights for black Americans wanted to discuss in the 1950s: the question of ethnoracial mixture.

To what extent are the borders between communities of descent to be maintained and why? The question is an old one of species-wide relevance, more demanding of critical study than ever at the start of the twenty-first century as more nations are diversified by migration, and as the inhibitions of the 1950s recede farther into the past. The history of this question in the United States invites special scrutiny because this country is one of the most conspicuously multi-descent nations in the industrialized North Atlantic West. The United States has served as a major site for engagement with the question, both behaviorally and discursively. Americans have mixed in certain ways and not others, and they have talked about it in certain ways and not others.

From 1958, I will look both backward and forward, drawing on recent scholarship to observe what the history of the United States looks like when viewed through the lens of our question. Certain truths come into sharper focus when viewed through this lens, and whatever instruction the case of the United States may afford to a world facing the prospect of increased mixture comes more fully into view.

Why were Arendt's contemporaries so eager to avoid the question of ethnoracial mixture? Because they had good reason to expect that any discussion of it would play into the hands of segregationists. Defenders of the Jim Crow system had been saying for years that the whole issue was race-mixing, anyway. All that civil rights agitation, they said, was an elaborate smoke screen for the simple truth, which was that black men wanted white women. School integration in particular was said to be a slippery slope if not a conspiracy: the mixing of black and white in the classroom would lead to more social contact, and ultimately to miscegenation.

Such charges on the part of segregationists would have been of less concern to the liberals were not so many other Americans, including an imposing number of white, northern opponents of segregation, dubious about marriage across the color line. A Gallup poll of that very year showed that 96 percent of white Americans disapproved of interracial marriage. This sentiment did not necessarily entail support for the remaining laws against black-white marriage still being enforced in Virginia and several other southern states, but it did mean that organizing to overturn such laws was not a priority.

Only nine years after the Arendt episode, to be sure, the Supreme Court ruled in the case of *Loving v. Virginia* that the Virginia statute was unconstitutional. Things moved quickly in the 1960s.[4] When Mildred and Richard Loving learned that a major civil rights bill was being debated in Congress, they were inspired to appeal their conviction. But black-white marriages were still against the law in every state but one south of the Mason-Dixon line as late as 1967, when the court's ruling in *Loving* ended legal restrictions on marriage across any and all color lines.[5] Thereafter, white opposition to black-white marriages diminished gradually but steadily, decade by decade.[6] Black-white marriages themselves remained rare, although they tripled in the quarter-century after the court's ruling.[7]

Yet Arendt understood more fully than did her exasperated friends that the Virginia statute's approach to the question of ethnoracial mixture was peculiarly American. Even the Union of South Africa did not have a miscegenation statute until 1949, and that one was based on the American model.[8] The notorious Nuremberg laws of Nazi Germany were, as Werner Sollors has pointed out, inspired partly by the miscegenation laws of the United States.[9] The cosmopolitan Arendt knew that racial restrictions on marriage were a real problem from a human rights point of view, and were a striking historical anomaly that American liberals were loath to face. The very word "miscegenation" was, after all, an American contribution to the English language.

Prior to the coining of this term during the Civil War, "amalgamation" had been the word generally used to refer to the mixing of races. This was true of Wendell Phillips and a handful of other abolitionists who did espouse the eventual mixing of the races as a goal,[10] and was true for alarmists warning against it. But in 1863, the very year emancipation made mixture more possible, "amalgamation" was replaced by the more ominous word that rang more like "mistaken mixture," and under circumstances not so different from those that surrounded Arendt nearly a century later. In an episode familiar to specialists in U.S. history but known to few other people today, *Miscegenation* was the title of an anonymous tract widely distributed in the North late in 1863 calling on the Republican Party to embrace the cause of race-mixing and make it the basis for that party's campaign of the following year. The tract was a hoax, written and distributed by two proslavery journalists who hoped to push the Republicans into endorsing this manifestly unpopular idea and thus to be more likely to lose the election to the Democrats. As Sidney Kaplan has demonstrated, the abolitionists themselves were suspicious from the start.[11] The abolitionists did not know the tract was a hoax until after the election, when Abraham Lincoln's success rendered the revelation of the hoax a minor footnote to the campaign. But all during the campaign, the Republicans apparently felt about the anonymous author much the same way liberals of 1958 felt about Arendt.

Eventually, miscegenation would become an ostensibly neutral word,[12] but one that flourished in a Jim Crow discourse alongside another term that came into use for the mixing of white Americans with each other. This was the notion of the "melting pot." It had been around since the earliest years of the Republic, but it gained currency at the start of the twentieth century in relation to massive immigration from Eastern and Southern Europe. This problematic figure of speech was used primarily to address the prospects for the incorporation of these predominantly Italian, Jewish, and Polish immigrants and their descendants, and not simply as ethnic groups within a plural society but as individuals who would as a matter of course intermarry with the British and other Northwestern European stocks. What made the term problematic was an ambiguity analyzed by Philip Gleason and others. Was the idea to melt down the immigrants and to then pour the resulting, formless liquid into preexisting cultural and social molds modeled on Anglo-Protestants like Henry Ford and Woodrow Wilson, or was the idea instead that everyone, Mayflower descendants and Sicilians and Irish and Ashkenazi and Slovaks, would act chemically upon each other so that all would be changed, and a new compound would emerge?[13]

Although both versions of the melting pot had their champions and their critics—and of course there were strong voices against both, preferring to keep out altogether any immigrants who were not "Nordic"—very few of the early twentieth-century discussants of the melting pot even mentioned blacks, for whom mixing with whites was "miscegenation."[14] Yet when Ralph Waldo Emerson had spoken before the Civil War about an American "smelting pot"—a slightly different figure of speech associated originally with the concept of amalgamation—he had explicitly included "Africans and Polynesians" in addition to "all the European tribes."[15] Not that Emerson's welcoming of people of all colors and from all continents was shared by that many of his white contemporaries. Quite the contrary. Emerson here spoke for a tiny minority. But he spoke in the idiom of melting, or smelting, before the vocabulary had changed. As the new word— miscegenation—became associated with black-white mixing, a preoccupation of the years after the Civil War, the residual European immigrant aspect of the question came to be more than ever a thing apart, discussed all the more easily without any reference to the African American aspect of the question. This separation of mixture talk into two discourses facilitated, and was in turn reinforced by, the process Matthew Frye Jacobson has detailed whereby European immigrant groups became less ambiguously white by becoming more and more definitively "not black."[16] The Jim Crow era featured not only separate schools and public accommodations in many states but also separate and invidious national vocabularies for talking about mixture.

The two vocabularies reflected the two historical conditions that make the United States the North Atlantic West's most dynamic site for dealing with our question. First, the United States operated under one of the few constitutional regimes in that domain that had tolerated slavery as recently as the 1860s and as a result had a national population a significant segment of which—about 12 percent during most of the twentieth century—was color-marked as once having been pieces of property or as being the direct descendants of people who had been.[17] Second, the United States was the most self-consciously immigrant-based society in all of Europe and North America, distinguished even from Canada by the proportion of its population derived from outside Great Britain and France and by the fact that Canada did not have a citizenship law to distinguish its own nationality from that of the British Empire until 1947. The foreign-born population of the United States between 1860 and 1930 ranged between 11.6 percent and 14.7 percent, and a much larger percentage than that of white inhabitants throughout those seventy years were, of course, the children or grandchildren of immigrants.

A third condition helps make the United States a setting in which our question is importantly engaged: the presence of Indians, or at least the presence of those indigenous people who were left after the slaughters and disease-caused deaths that accompanied the occupation of their land by Europeans. Yet the Indian case was sufficiently different from both the African American case and that of the European immigrants to stand somewhat outside the miscegenation conversation and the melting pot conversation. Indians had been enslaved episodically in the British colonies of North America, but Indian slavery was never a significant feature of labor systems in the United States. Twelve states did include Indians in their miscegenation statutes, but enforcement was often lax. The Virginia law did not include Indians because a motion to include them was defeated by Tidewater aristocrats who claimed to be the descendants of John Rolfe and Pocahontas. For all the anti-Indian behavior and attitudes on the part of the white population, the latter often nourished an idealized view of the "noble savage," which historians have shown coexisted with the most genocidal of dispositions. Millions of white Americans have bragged that they had "Indian blood," and often cited it by quantum, as in "I'm one-eighth Cherokee." The appropriation of Indian land was accompanied by an extensive appropriation of the Indian genetic heritage and Indian symbolic identification with America. The topic of white-Indian mixture was most often discussed in terms of blood quantum, not only by federal officials but also by tribal governments and in everyday conversation on the part of whites.[18]

The affirmation of Indian ancestry proceeds apace in our own time. In the twenty years between 1970 and 1990, the federal census reported an increase of 259 percent in the American Indian population despite a very low birthrate. What had happened, of course, is that more and more Americans decided to "come out" as part Indian.[19] The American Indian population, even as expanded, remains a tiny fraction of the nation—about 1 percent— but it demands mention on account of the contrast it presents to the African American case. We do not see a multitude of ostensibly white Americans reclassifying themselves as part black.[20]

The stigma carried by blackness is unique, and is affixed and perpetuated resolutely by the American practice of treating blackness as a monolithic identity that an individual either has or does not have on the basis of the principle that any African ancestry at all determines that one is simply black.[21] The invidiousness of this "one-drop rule" was eloquently encapsulated by Barbara Fields more than twenty years ago: we have a convention "that considers a white woman capable of giving birth to a black child but denies that a black woman can give birth to a white child."[22] One has not been able to say, "I'm one-eighth African American" without giving up socially, if not legally, the seven-eighths part of one's self that is not. You can be one-eighth Cherokee and still be seven-eighths something else, but if you are one-eighth black you are not likely to be counted as white at all. Indeed, one index of the power of the one-drop rule for blacks is that some Indian tribal governments have recently tried to expel from tribal membership long-time members who have demonstrably black ancestors.[23]

Comparativists have often commented on the uniqueness to the United States of this principle of hypodescent.[24] The principle is widely taken for granted in the United States right down to the present, and is even defended as a political strategy in some contexts by organizations speaking for the interests of African Americans.[25] But the principle originates in the property interests of slaveholders. Children begotten upon slave women by their owners or by other white men would grow up as slaves, adding to the property of the owners of the women and preserving the amazingly durable fiction that male slaveholders and the other white males in the vicinity were faithful to their wives. The principle was sharpened during the Jim Crow era, when opposition to social equality for blacks was of course well served by a monolithic notion of blackness accompanied by legislation that outlawed as miscegenation black-white marriages but left less strictly regulated any non-marital sex in which white males might engage with black females. As Tocqueville famously remarked well before the Civil War, "To debauch a Negro girl hardly injures an American's reputation; to marry her dishonors him."[26]

Some of the slave era and Jim Crow regimes did employ fractional classifications, providing that "Octoroons," "Quadroons," and "Mulattos" be separately counted and allowed distinctive rights and privileges in some jurisdictions.[27] But this fractional approach was hard to administer, invited litigation, and blurred lines that many whites wanted kept sharp. In 1894, Mark Twain's *Pudd'nhead Wilson* mocked a law that stipulated $1/32$ as the fraction of black ancestry that decided one's race.[28] "Mulatto" was dropped from the federal census after 1920, and more and more state governments went the way of the Virginia statute, which as revised in 1924 classified as white only a person "who has no trace whatsoever of blood other than Caucasian."[29]

Criticism of this one-drop rule has surfaced from time to time,[30] but not until the 1990s did critical discussion of hypodescent become sustained and widespread in mainstream media. The lead in this discussion was taken by persons at least some of whose white ancestry derives from recent voluntary unions rather than from the legacy of the exploitation of slave women by white masters and overseers.[31] But at stake is the degree of identity choice available to all black individuals whose measure of whiteness has been erased by law and convention. At stake, too, is the extent to which the United States as a whole will finally acknowledge the reality of the black-white mixing that has already taken place, and will thus be obliged to accept a fact long recognized by scholars: that blackness in the United States is an ascribed status, imposed on a spectrum of color shades and descent percentages, rather than a category of nature.[32] At stake, further and most important, is the significance of blackness itself in this society. While there is a danger that the acceptance of mixture will ultimately reinforce white privilege by treating as "white" all but the darkest, who might then be all the more isolated and subject to enduring prejudice, isn't there also a more hopeful prospect? The more that mixture is accepted, the less fear there might be of what is being mixed. Blackness itself might become less stigmatized. If the one-drop rule is an indicator of the depth of anti-black racism, might not the weakening of that rule be an indicator of the diminution of that racism? The present historical moment differs from previous episodes of "whiting" in that now the very white-black distinction is being critically engaged rather than reinforced and sharpened in the process of being relocated to render Jews, Italians, Mexicans, and others more clearly white and blacks more clearly black.

The vigorous debate over the census classifications—should there be a box to check for mixed race, should an individual be able to check more than one box, and so forth—is only the most visible aspect of an unprecedented discursive episode in the history of American engagement with our question. A society that often has policed the black-white color line with terror now registers a more relaxed fascination with the crossing of that line, even widespread acceptance of such crossings. Hollywood movies explore the theme with increasing frequency, and family memoirs of black-white fusion fill the display tables at bookstores. Some of these books—including James McBride's *The Color of Water* and Shirlee Taylor Haizlip's *The Sweeter the Juice*—have become best-sellers.[33] And among recent fiction bestsellers, Philip Roth's *The Human Stain* gives us the most artistically and morally ambitious treatment of black-white mixing and of the multiple paradoxes of the one-drop rule offered by a white novelist since Mark Twain.[34] Organizations lobbying for greater recognition of ethnoracial mixture proliferate, sponsor conferences, publish volume after volume, and now operate numerous web sites.[35] DNA evidence lending support to the old suspicion that Thomas Jefferson fathered children with a slave mistress has stimulated sympathetic retellings of the Jefferson–Sally Hemings story that help mark the difference between our time and even the very recent past, when the mere mention of Hemings was often received as a scurrilous attack on Jefferson's honor. Tellers of the Jefferson-Hemings story now explore more readily the possibility that the relationship was a tender and loving one, and sometimes imply that the relation-ship, despite the horrors of slavery, illustrates the way in which American society is a single, extended family.[36] One journalist after another takes as a harbinger for the nation's demographic and ideological future the determination of the popular golf champion Tiger Woods to affirm all aspects of his multiple ances-try, including black, white, Indian, Chinese, and Thai.[37]

Oprah Winfrey proclaimed the mixed-descent Woods to be "America's son" in a construction that invites a comparison between what Woods' "family tree" might look like and the family tree of another "America's son," the one drawn by Norman Rock-well at about the time of Hannah Arendt's imbroglio with *Com-mentary* and the Lovings' arrest in Virginia. Rockwell's "Family Tree," offered as the *Saturday Evening Post* cover for October 24, 1959, is defined by a preoccupation with degrees of respectability and with Union-Confederate reconciliation, not by the mixing of ethnoracial groups. (See Figure 1.) Rockwell shows the stylized,

Figure 1. "Family Tree" by Norman Rockwell. Copyright 1959 SEPS. Licensed by Curtis Publishing, Indianapolis, Indiana. All rights reserved. www.curtispublishing.com.

Ozzie-and-Harriet era white child to be the descendant of, among other characters, a colonial-era pirate and frontier-based "Squaw man" and their mates. There is no black face on the tree, but Rockwell invites beholders, while chuckling at their culture's tendency for genealogical aggrandizement, to be comfortable with the Indian woman in the Anglo child's genealogy, as well as with the presence there of a proto-Latina in the person of the pirate's mate.[38] The whiteness of the cherubic little boy at the top of the painting filters visually down the tree—and back through American history—to cover all the people Rockwell admits into the company of begetters and begotten. The men whose social marginality is marked by their non-Anglo mates are thus recognized in the family tree of the white 1950s, as are even the slightly darker women who coupled with the one-eyed pirate and the scruffy frontiersman. Rockwell's "Family Tree" is a super-Anglo picture of the American population, in which tiny quantities of Hispanic and Indian descent are feminized, located in a distant past, and diluted to the point of non-recognition in Rockwell's white present. Had Rockwell been more concerned to display an ethnoracially marked melting pot, he might well have rendered some of the more swarthy figures in the picture easily recognized as non-Anglo European immigrants. But the evident lack of such an intent on Rockwell's part renders his inclusion of the Indian and the *senorita/senora* all the more revealingly incidental. It was inconceivable that Rockwell would have encouraged the white readers of the *Saturday Evening Post* in 1959 to suppose that a black person might be among their ancestors, but it was not a stretch to get Indians and Latinos into the mix.

But the ancestry of Tiger Woods also includes Chinese and Thai. Woods' partly Asian ancestry can direct us to one of the circumstances that have promoted the extraordinary new display of interest in the question of ethnoracial mixture in our own time and can turn us, also, to dimensions of the question involving Americans of Asian and Latin American descent.

Massive immigration from Asia and Latin America since about 1970 has radically altered the ethnoracial composition of the United States, has produced new kinds of mixtures, and by enacting socially recognized mixture on a large scale has made some African Americans all the more cognizant of the invidious character of the one-drop rule for black identity.[39] We get a sense of the magnitude of this new migration if we contemplate the fact that the number of non-black immigrants between 1970 and 2000 who are also non-Europeans roughly equals the number of African Americans already resident in the United States in 1980, about 26 million. Another 9 million non-black immigrants entered the United States during the same three decades, especially from Russia, Ukraine, Poland, and Iran (a "Middle Eastern" rather than an "Asian" country by popular reckoning), but the Asian and Latin American migrations were the most relevant to our question. Each of these two cases had features that distinguished it from the other, and from the African American case to which both are often compared.

Immigrants from Asia were entering a country with only a tiny number of preexisting Asian Americans—there were only about a million and a half at the time of the Celler Act in 1965, well under 1 percent of the population—yet a country with a history of anti-Asian prejudice that in some respects ran parallel to anti-black prejudice, even legally, and in other respects did not. The Chinese Exclusion Act of 1882 was the first nationally or ethnoracially group-specific restriction on immigration, and Asian immigrants generally remained ineligible to become naturalized citizens until 1952, when Congress finally abolished the white-only principle for naturalization that had been in place since 1790 and that courts had subsequently construed to apply to immigrants from India as well from East Asia.[40] Asians were never constitutionally enslaved, nor were they lynched in large numbers in the twentieth century, but some of the miscegenation statutes listed "Oriental" or "Mongolian" along with "Negro."[41] In southern states, this followed less from the presence of Asian ethnics—there were almost none in most southern states—than from doctrinal consistency.

Only in a few western states, especially California, was the prohibition of marriages between whites and Asians a serious project. Yet even California's miscegenation statute had been ruled unconstitutional by that state's own supreme court in 1948, nearly twenty years before *Loving v. Virginia* and even more distant from the new wave of immigrants from China, Korea, Vietnam, India, and other Asian nations that began to appear. By the time of that immigration, moreover, most white Americans who had an opinion about Japanese internment during World War II, the most notorious enactment of anti-Asian prejudice in popular memory, regarded that internment as a dreadful mistake, deserving even of reparations, which were in fact eventually paid.[42]

Hence the new immigrants from Asia were entering the country at a time when anti-Asian prejudice was in decline and when restrictions on Asian-white marriages were a distant memory in the parts of the country where most Asians had been living and where most of the new immigrants settled. These circumstances— taken together with the fact that many of the new immigrants from Asia had vibrant international kinship networks and marketable skills that quickly translated into strong class position—help explain the rapid incorporation of Asian ethnics into American society, even as measured by intermarriage. In the 1990 census, about half of the Asian Americans who had been born in the United States and were then getting married were acquiring non-Asian spouses.[43] The high rate of Asian-white marriage blurs the line between these two descent communities, and thus speaks to the question of ethnoracial mixture behaviorally by exemplifying the relative ease of mixture even for a non-European group against which miscegenation laws were once on the books and members of which were thrown into concentration camps without a shred of due process even within my own lifetime.[44]

The expansion through immigration of the Hispanic or Latino descent community, too, speaks behaviorally to the question
of ethnoracial mixture in a highly different context, yet in terms
that eventually proved almost as challenging to the habit of taking
the African American case as a model for understanding and responding to the injustices done to other ethnoracially defined
minorities. Part of what it meant to be Latino to begin with constituted a challenge to the American system of classification, because the category was less strictly color-marked. Immigrants from
Mexico, by far the largest Latin American producer of immigrants to the United States, were understood to derive from two
descent communities classified as races in the United States: Caucasian and Indian. The mixing of Spanish colonials from Europe
with the indigenous population of the New World generated the
notion of mestizo. The more Mexican Americans in the United
States, as Gary Nash has observed, the less relevant were the old
"racial" categories.[45]

This mixing of European and indigenous blood did not prevent the Latino population of the Southwest from being abused by
Anglos, who found the Latinos different enough whatever they
were made of. Segregated schools were common in the 1920s and
1930s in Texas, California, and Arizona. Texas citizens of Mexican descent were routinely prevented from serving on juries until
1954, when the U.S. Supreme Court ruled, in *Hernandez v. Texas*,
that the Fourteenth Amendment rights of Hispanics, even though
said to be "white" by the state of Texas, were violated when Hispanics were excluded as a "class" from service on juries. Yet none
of the miscegenation statutes mention Latinos by any of the
names they might have been called. Latinos were usually regarded
as legally white even when being stigmatized and mistreated. In
court cases under miscegenation law, persons said by opposing
counsel to be Negro, as Peggy Pascoe has shown, often insisted that
they were actually Mexican. Much then depended on a court's assessment of the "pedigree," as it was often put, of a person whose

marriage was under threat of annulment on the grounds of the alleged discovery of a partly black ancestry.[46] The understanding that to be Mexican was to be legally white was so taken for granted in some settings that the plaintiff in the California suit that resulted in the invalidating of that state's miscegenation statute was herself a Mexican American. Andrea Perez, both of whose parents had been born in Mexico, sued several Los Angeles County clerks for declining to issue a marriage license enabling her to marry a man who was black, whom she met on the assembly line in her capacity as a "Rosie the Riveter." (See Figure 2.) Right in the heart of the history of our question, then, in the pathbreaking case on which *Loving v. Virginia* was modeled, Latinos were sufficiently Caucasian that Perez's Mexican ancestry was not even mentioned in the case's documents and was rarely noted in newspapers other than those published by and for African Americans.[47] *Perez v. Sharp* is a reminder of how different California was from the states of the former Confederacy: its state supreme court actually threw out a miscegenation statute, and it did so a full decade before the Lovings were arrested and Hannah Arendt shocked New York liberals with her interest in the issue.[48] The situation was somewhat different in Texas, where Andrea Perez might well have been allowed to marry a black man. Mexicans "were rarely, if ever prosecuted" when they married blacks, as Neil Foley has explained, because Mexicans, while legally white, were "often regarded as nonwhite." Yet many "middle class Texas Mexicans," Foley summarizes, were eventually able to move "out of the ethnoracial borderlands between blackness and whiteness by constructing identities as Americans and embracing whiteness" because they, unlike African Americans, were not "racially marked as black" by "the so-called one-drop rule."[49]

Even in California, however, Mexican Americans had not been considered white when they wanted to marry Asians. Thus quite a number of Punjabi immigrants acquired Mexican American spouses in the 1920s and 1930s because county clerks enforced

Figure 2. Andrea Perez in a 1982 staff photo, from Morningside Elementary School in Pacoima, California, where Perez worked as a bilingual teacher's aide while in her sixties. Photo courtesy of Dara Orenstein and Morningside Elementary School District. Perez was the plaintiff in the case that struck down California's miscegenation law in 1948 and set the frame for *Loving v. Virginia*. She met her black husband-to-be while working in an airplane assembly plant during World War II and remained married to him until her death in 2000.

the state's prohibition on Asian-white marriages only when the Asian Indians sought to marry Anglos. This anomaly is rendered all the more striking by the fact that the South Asian immigrants were technically Caucasian according to classic race theory, but in 1923 were declared by the U.S. Supreme Court to be non-white anyway.[50]

Yet the federal government was eventually obliged to recognize that some Latinos were on the black side of the black-white color line. Puerto Ricans and immigrants from Cuba and the Dominican Republic, for example, grew up in societies that did not mark the black-white color line sharply, with the result that, in the words adopted by the Census Bureau in 1970, "Hispanics can be of any race." This simple declarative, designed to acknowledge that some people the government classified as racially black were socially and culturally identified with Latin America, was remarkable in several respects. It subtly compromised the principle of hypodescent for blacks. It left intact the notion that white and black were racial rather than ethnic categories and that there was an important distinction between race and ethnicity. And it produced the awkward, antiphonal census category of "non-Hispanic white."[51] Thus the Bureau of the Census ended up designating the white majority of the whole country not by a label designed specifically for it but by referring to what that majority was not. It is as if the only term one had for British people from outside Wales was "non-Welsh British."

The Latino case had other peculiarities. Latinos shared with Asian Americans a history free of legally recognized slavery within the United States, but, unlike immigrants from Asia, their immigration had not been decisively restricted. Mexicans, whose naturalization rights had been guaranteed by treaty in 1848 and whose inexpensive agricultural labor was sought by landowners in the Southwest, had been exempted from the epochal Immigration Restriction Act of 1924 that ended the massive immigration from Eastern and Southern Europe and made more rigid the exclusions of Asians that were already in place. Despite the resulting migration across the border, however, only 4.5 percent of the American population were Hispanic as registered by the census of 1970.[52]

That figure had gone up to 12.5 percent by 2000, thus bringing into much greater prominence a "racially" mixed community of descent that some Latino advocates insisted should be called a "race" of its own, subject to abandoning the biological understanding of race and replacing it with a more cultural one.[53] It is no wonder the government resisted this move, because if the race-ethnicity distinction were broken in the direction of classifying Latinos as a race, where else might this move lead? Were Jews, too, a race after all, because the Nazis, even if they got the theory wrong, managed to get the word right? What about Arabs? Armenians? Irish? Many scholars have long since adopted the terms "ethnoracial," "communities of descent," and "racialized groups" to refer to what were once called either "races" or "ethnic groups," recognizing the blurred, contingent, and constructed character of the relevant boundaries, but the Census Bureau and much of the American public remains in the thrall of the concept of race.[54]

In the meantime, more and more of the already mixed Latinos were getting married to non-Latinos. By the 1990 census, nearly one-third of Latinos born in the United States who were getting married were out-marrying.[55] By 2000, it was clearer than ever that out-marriage for Latinos increased with the number of years north of the border, and with levels of education and income. The Latinos least likely to out-marry were the most poorly educated of recent immigrants (often illegal) and their children, whose chances of getting ahead were diminished by the decay of the public school system and other public services in California and elsewhere in the Southwest. The Latino case thus confirms the implications of the Asian American case that class position exercises enormous influence over the relative stability of ethnoracial boundaries.

That the weak class position of most African Americans owes much to the legacy of slavery and Jim Crow has long been understood, but the formidable role of miscegenation law in that legacy is not widely appreciated. The defense of slaves as property is what inspired not only hypodescent but also miscegenation law itself as first developed in the Chesapeake colonies during the seventeenth century. The governments of the slave-intensive colonies and their successor states did not try very hard to prevent the birth of children with black mothers and white fathers, but they did act to make it difficult for the children of such unions to achieve any right to inheritance. As Eva Saks has established on the basis of an analysis of the entire history of the relevant court cases, fear of property loss was a driving force behind the prohibition on black-white marriage. And so it remained right down to the Civil War. Emancipation deprived the white southerners of their property in the form of slave chattels, but these white southerners could protect much of the rest of their property and re-create some of the social and economic conditions of slavery by preventing most descendants of black-white sexual unions from advancing inheritance claims. The ex-Confederates did this by legally marking all of the issue of their former slaves as permanently and exclusively black and by prohibiting any black person from marrying a white person. Hence all children of black-white couplings were bastards, and under the law in many jurisdictions they had no claim to inheritance. Jim Crow-era legislators and judges, as Saks shows, knew full well what was at stake. Six of the Reconstruction state governments had repealed the miscegenation statutes of the slave era, but as soon as the Republicans withdrew federal power in 1877—not to deliver it again for eighty years, when President Eisenhower did it at Little Rock—the former slaveholders and their allies regained control, and promptly reenacted and sharpened the slave era's prohibitions on black-white marriage.[56]

The combination of hypodescent with the denial to blacks residing in many states with large black populations of any opportunity for legal marriage to whites ensured that the color line would long remain to a very large extent a property line. Hence the dynamics of *race* formation and the dynamics of *class* formation were, in this most crucial of all American cases, largely the same. This is one of the most important truths about the history of the United States brought into sharper focus when that history is viewed through the lens of the question of ethnoracial mixture.

In the context of this truth, it cannot be repeated often enough that miscegenation law generally treated Latinos as white, and it was applied with little consistency to Indians and Asians. To be sure, marital and legal reproductive freedoms for Indians and Asian Americans were restricted in some states for a number of years. But these restrictions did not perpetuate the social and economic conditions of slavery, and thus had a less profound effect on class position. Moreover, the bulk of the Latino and Asian American population of the United States today are either immigrants or the children of immigrants, not the descendants of families who were directly affected by the miscegenation laws of state governments within the United States. To recognize these differences is not to obscure the injustice inflicted on non-black descent groups, which historians have amply documented. But it is to confront the peculiar circumstances, duration, and class-consolidating consequences of anti-black racism. The power of this particular variety of racism to perform such extreme racialization and economic domination derived from the fact that black people, and they alone, were overwhelmingly the descendants of men and women who had been pieces of property in the British colonies and in the United States, and that these black people, unlike immigrants of all colors, even those from Mexico, had little choice but to reside in the country in which their ancestors had been enslaved, and that they, unlike Indians, carried no mystique of the new American Eden.

Yet these differences in the historical experience of the several American minority descent groups sometimes have been hidden from view as we react in horror to the evils of white racism whole-sale. This happened during the 1960s when the nation's system of anti-racist programs was organized and during the 1970s when these programs were consolidated and the political alliances supporting these programs were cemented. At those historical moments, significantly, almost nobody wanted to look at the society and history of the United States through the lens of our question.

Legal and educational initiatives primarily designed with African Americans in mind were extended to other historically disadvantaged ethnoracial minorities, implicitly color-coded as yellow, brown, and red. People in each of these color groups had been dreadfully mistreated, after all, and were still the victims of prejudice in many contexts. It was convenient to apply to those groups the basic approach already worked out for black Americans. As John D. Skrentny has shown, the assumption that this or that group was "like blacks" drove the "minority rights revolution" in certain directions, while the failure of the black analogy to gain credibility in relation to some other classes of well-mobilized disadvantaged persons limited the scope of that revolution.[57]

Although the decision to expand the range of Affirmative Action beyond the black population was taken in the 1960s by government bureaucrats with little pressure from political organizations devoted to advancing the interests of Asian Americans, Latinos, and Indians, such organizations usually welcomed these expansions once effected, and in the 1970s they became forces behind the defense of Affirmative Action programs. A conglomerate of minority advocacy organizations seemed like a good political investment. And at exactly the time that these lobby groups and the governmental and educational officials who responded to their concerns were acting, black Americans were asserting themselves vigorously as a group, showing more interest in group solidarity than in the problematic character of the one-drop rule. The black model as understood in the early 1970s—by African American advocacy organizations as well as by public officials and courts—carried the assumption of sharp group boundaries as facts of life and did not offer a challenge to such boundaries as historically contingent constructions.[58] Indeed, to proceed otherwise was potentially to deny to victims of white racism the benefits they were due: if the one-drop rule defined discrimination, it naturally defined anti-discrimination remedies.

What came to be called Affirmative Action and multiculturalism were both predicated on the sense that ethnoracial groups were clearly bounded, durable entities. This sense was strongly reinforced throughout the 1970s by negative representations of the very ideal of assimilation, which as supervised by Anglo-Protestants was said to have robbed immigrant groups, especially Catholics from Ireland, Poland, and Italy, of their cultural heritage. Michael Novak's 1971 bestseller, *The Rise of the Unmeltable Ethnics,* gave voice to the notion that what really called for defense was the integrity of groups rather than the opportunity to cross the boundaries between them.[59] In 1972, Congress passed the Ethnic Heritage Studies Act, providing federal funds for programs that would study the culture of ethnic groups. Sociologists sometimes interpreted this upsurge of European ethnicities as largely a symbolic affirmation of old world images facilitated by the very extent of the assimilation experienced by the ethnicity-affirming populations, and asserted that the upsurge was in some respects a "backlash" against official attention to the needs of black people.[60] Yet these anti-assimilationist, culturally particularist gestures on the part of many European-derived descent groups rendered all the more credible the multiculturalist and Affirmative Action initiatives that played to the enduring integrity of each community of descent. Educational initiatives as well as entitlement programs were better able to get moving if one supposed the society to be divided up in easily managed, often color-coded groups, each possessed of its own culture.[61]

But in this wholesome rush to recognize diversity while reducing it to a manageable set of monoliths, questions that later proved to be important were not asked. As Skrentny, Hugh Davis Graham, and other scholars have documented, the officials who added one group or another to the list of those targeted for a particular entitlement provided few explanations for their often sweeping directives and rulings, held almost no public hearings to air the issues, and generally failed to think through the theoretical basis of their decisions.[62] Just what groups should benefit from group-specific entitlements and on the basis of what justification? What specific characteristics marked an individual as a member of a designated group? What was the significance of mixed descent? Were new immigrants as eligible as the descendants of slaves, and, if so, on the basis of what analysis of the relation of their particular descent community to the prior and present actions of the United States and its citizens?

As a result of the failure to address these questions, especially the last one, 26 million Asian and Latin American immigrants and their children eventually found themselves eligible for at least some Affirmative Action benefits simply by virtue of the fact that they had come from Panama or Taiwan or the Philippines rather than from Iraq or Greece or Russia. There was virtually no public debate on the issue of immigrant eligibility for ethnoracially defined entitlements. Political opponents of Affirmative Action sometimes called attention to examples of well-to-do, highly educated immigrants taking up minority set-aside business contracts in programs that had won approval on the grounds that they would assist American-born blacks. But the intent was almost always to undermine all of Affirmative Action rather than to distinguish between its justification for blacks and its justification for immigrants and their children.[63] Federal agencies and courts—along with many multicultural education programs carrying out "affirmative action for cultures"—operated on the basis of an implicit calculus of victimization, but they shrank from the task of following through, of actually developing the calculus and offering it for public scrutiny.

To be sure, the pivotal political and administrative decisions were taken when the population of Asian Americans and Latinos was tiny—less than 1 percent of Americans were listed as of Asian descent in the census of 1970, and only 4.5 percent were Latinos—and before officials, civil rights leaders, and policy intellectuals had any inkling that the Immigration and Nationality Act of 1965 would produce so many immigrants from Asia and Latin America. Had the Asian American and Latino populations remained as steady as the African American population, the extension of entitlements to these other groups might not have put the system under such pressure. But the millions of ethnoracially Asian and Latino immigrants revolutionized the meaning of descent-defined entitlements. The number of Americans potentially eligible for at least some Affirmative Action programs more than doubled even during the decades that Affirmative Action for American-born blacks was under increasing political pressure, and even as the relative ease with which the children of immigrants from Asia and Latin America mixed with Americans of European descent shattered the myth that all non-European ethnoracial groups in America were as tightly bounded as the black group, whose borders were kept tidy by the historically anomalous practice of hypodescent racialization.

Perhaps an intellectually coherent and politically viable argument could have been developed for entitlement programs for non-blacks, including some newly arriving immigrants. There was no shortage of abuses to be enumerated and assessed, nor was evidence lacking that many whites were prejudiced against persons of Asian or Latin American descent. White privilege was real, and there were good reasons to design programs to combat its power. But such an argument on behalf of policies serving non-blacks was not developed with sufficient specificity to preserve the special claims of African Americans, whose interests virtually all policymakers in the 1960s assumed was the point of the entire entitlement conversation.[64] Hence later on, when immigrant eligibility for Affirmative Action programs exposed the entire system of ethnoracially targeted entitlements to be a jerry-built, poorly theorized edifice quite different from what President Lyndon Johnson and his Great Society associates had in mind, and no longer subject to viable defense on the powerful grounds of the distinctive history of African Americans, it was too late to save Affirmative Action for African Americans except on the piecemeal basis to which political pressures of several kinds had reduced it by the end of the 1990s.

In the meantime, defenders of Affirmative Action rarely focused on immigrant eligibility for entitlement programs, and concentrated instead on charging opponents of Affirmative Action with trying to perpetuate white privilege. No doubt this charge was often true, but this emphasis in the defense of Affirmative Action also dodged the increasing complexity of the actual politics in which group preferences were embedded.[65] The edifice of ethnoracially defined entitlements had been designed architecturally by practical bureaucrats who did not foresee the potential scope of the edifice's operations; then, the political defense of the edifice against those who would dismantle it was taken up by a multigroup coalition that tried to make the old design work despite increasingly apparent differences among the groups the edifice had come to serve.

A major consequence of this post-1960s episode in mixture avoidance and minority group equivalency was that the American public gradually lost its grip on an insight that had been prominent when the Civil Rights Act of 1964 and the Voting Rights Act of 1965 were passed by large, bipartisan majorities in both the Senate and the House of Representatives. That insight was that the descent community of African Americans was historically unique. Only blacks inherit a multi-century legacy of group-specific enslavement and hypodescent racialization long carried out under constitutional authority in the United States. But the monolithic character of white racism has been so taken for granted that white racism has been assigned the same capacity often assigned to a single drop of black blood: the capacity to define equally whatever it touched, no matter how the affected entity was constituted and what its life circumstances might have been. We might call it the principle of white racist hypovictimization, or the one hate rule. To become aware of the one hate rule's ironic relation to the one-drop rule is not to imply that the damage done by honest efforts to combat white racism by treating it monolithically is remotely on the same scale as the damage done by hypodescent racialization. But this irony is another feature of the history of the United States that comes into clearer focus when that history is seen through the lens of the question of ethnoracial mixture.[66]

There is yet more to see through the lens of our question if we hold our gaze a bit longer and broaden its scope. By looking back from recent census data on the whole sweep of American history, prepared now to discern mixture even where it was denied by historical actors, we can see unfolding a human drama for which the vocabulary of the melting pot is not adequate, nor that of miscegenation, nor that of blood quantum. The concept of "assimilation," too, is insufficient, not only on account of its implication of a one-way process of newcomers adapting to an unchanging, prior society but also because the concept as commonly understood does not incorporate the prodigious black-white mixing masked by hypodescent racialization.[67] Nor do the recently popular, ahistorical figures of speech, "mosaic" or "salad bowl," begin to capture the decidedly temporal, dialectical drama that should be recognized as a major theme in the history of the United States, and that should again be called by its proper name: amalgamation.

That drama of amalgamation is behind the 1990 census reports I have already mentioned, indicating out-marriage rates for young Latinos born in the United States at about 33 percent and for Asian Americans at about 50 percent.[68] On the same charts, the out-marriage rate for American Indians is about 60 percent.

The experience of the European descent communities who entered the United States in large numbers during the great 1880–1924 migration is also highly pertinent. By the 1990s, persons who identified themselves as having Italian ancestry were acquiring spouses without any such ancestry at a rate of 73 percent, according to demographer Reynolds Farley, and the comparable figure for those with Polish ancestry was 81 percent.[69] Further from descent-group boundary maintenance are the descendants of the even earlier generations of migrants from Ireland, Germany, and Scandinavia. Further still are the descendants of immigrants from England, Scotland, and Wales, the subdivisions of Great Britain that once seemed important to Anglo-Americans. These varieties of white assimilation are often taken for granted as we contemplate the very different experience of non-European descent communities, but in world-historical perspective this mixing of Europeans, too, is far from trivial.

The case of Jewish Americans invites special attention in view of the fact that Jews, more than Italians and Poles, and the other groups who comprised the migration from Eastern and Southern Europe, were subject to extensive, legally sanctioned discrimination in housing, public accommodations, education, and employment as recently as World War II. In 1940, Jewish Americans were marrying non-Jews at a rate of about 3 percent but, by 1990, were doing so at a rate of well over 50 percent.[70] Since Jewish Americans have very strong class position, their experience can remind us, once again, that class position often advances or retards rates of intermarriage.

The Census Bureau tells us that only about 6 percent of African Americans—defined by the hypodescent standard—were acquiring non-black spouses by 1990.[71] The final report on this aspect of the 2000 census is yet to be released, but preliminary assessments place the figure at about 10 percent.[72] Why is the black out-marriage rate so much lower today than the rate for other ethnoracial minorities? Although weak class position on the part of most blacks and an enduring prejudice against blacks on the part of most whites are no doubt prominent factors, and would fit with most of the sociological theory on the dynamics of mixture, there is surely more to it than that. Some blacks have their own reasons for seeking black spouses. This can be true for any community of descent, as internal community adhesives are often compelling. But there are obvious historical reasons why some American blacks, as opposed to members of groups based on immigration, might want as little as possible to do with American whites, today and perhaps for a very long time into the future.[73]

Yet when we look at the statistics, we cannot fail to notice that the rate of black-white marriage is now considerably greater— several times greater—than the rate of Jewish-gentile marriage only sixty years ago. And we need to remember that not everyone who cohabits and reproduces gets married. The percentage of the American population—white and black, and even yellow and brown and red—that is getting married at all is diminishing. Non-marital cohabitation across ethnoracial lines is generally believed to be even more common than marriage across ethnoracial lines, but the data is less definitive.

Even so, the extent of ethnoracial mixing registered in the marriage statistics of the federal censuses of 1990 and 2000, taken together with the growing willingness to accept as real the black-white mixing—including that created by the massive rape of slave females—that has gone into the genetic making of the African American population, invites us to see the history of the United States as, among other things, a story of amalgamation, however episodic and however given to the greater bonding of some elements than others. To speak of "amalgamation" as a major theme in U.S. history is to reclaim the vocabulary of Wendell Phillips and Frederick Douglass and Ralph Waldo Emerson, to renounce the Jim Crow distinction between miscegenation and the melting pot, to integrate the story of black-white mixing with the story of other kinds of mixing, to escape the implications of Anglo-conformity often historically associated with the figure of the melting pot, to recognize a dynamic interaction not captured by the more limited concept of assimilation, and to deny at long last the legitimacy of the principle of hypodescent.

Amalgamation in the history of the United States has been episodic and segmented. Not every tribe in the United States has mixed equally with each other, or at the same pace, or with equal agency, or has faced the same obstacles and inhibitions and incentives and disincentives. Not every mixture has had an equal impact on the whole. Hence the old myth of the melting pot is at once deeply false and deeply true. To confront these features of the process of amalgamation and to understand the specific role played in that process by hypodescent racialization is to integrate the story of physical mixing with the story of racism and anti-racism. It is a mistake to treat these two narratives as rivals, with the story of physical mixing allowed to license political complacency ("We don't need policies to deal with the effects of racism, because we can just let nature take its course"), and the story of racism and anti-racism allowed to license calls for struggle ("We must mobilize to defeat racism"). The greater acceptance of descent mixture in our own time is obviously a result of the political struggle that has diminished racism in the United States. Its emergence cannot be explained apart from that struggle for ethnoracial equality.

The national experience with intimacy across ethnoracial lines has been one of amalgamation *interruptus:* irregular, stutter-step, tension-filled, and sometimes violent, and thus quite different from the spontaneous, relatively relaxed intimacy leading to closure so often celebrated under the sign of the melting pot. But it has been amalgamation nevertheless, and on a scale and within a time frame that gives it a strong claim to being one of the central features of the history of the United States when viewed in comparative perspective. A number of other nations have experienced large measures of mixture. Brazil, Argentina, South Africa, New Zealand, and Canada are prominent examples, each with its own history of our question deserving of the world's attention. But the United States is at least an important case in which a large number of descent groups deriving from a great range of points of origin have blended. If demographic mixture is a theme more prominent in the modern history of the Western Hemisphere than of the Eastern, the amalgamation narrative foregrounds the features of the United States that most make it an "American" nation rather than an expansion of a Europe in which nationality and descent continue to go together more often than not.[74]

This mixture-centered view of the history of the United States contrasts vividly with what is at once the most Western Hemisphere–preoccupied and the most conspicuously census-inspired of all interpretations of American history, the frontier thesis. Frederick Jackson Turner developed this interpretation on the basis of the census of 1890 finding that what had been the territory beyond white settlements was now made up of organized counties with enough people in them to be enumerated in the census. This led Turner to reflect on the significance of uninhabited land, which he declared to be the fostering of the individualism and democracy that, he believed, had made the United States what it was. The narrative of the frontier was keyed by the encounter of Europeans with a geographical environment defined by the absence of people. Indians did not really count as people, as their land was uninhabited by Turner's definition.[75] Yet the narrative of amalgamation is antithetical: it is keyed instead by the encounter of human beings with each other, across the lines of many communities of descent, in a series of intimacies and counterintimacies fostered by a range of economic and cultural forces.

Hence I invoke Turner not because his ideas are sufficiently alive today to demand refutation, nor to suggest that amalgamation and hypodescent are strong enough concepts to perform the range of analytic tasks Turner and his disciples asked the concept of the frontier to perform, but simply to underscore the difference between Turner's historiographical era and ours. The narrative of the frontier was remarkable for avoiding people and the specific terms of their action upon each other. The frontier thesis purported to explain the course of American history without much attention to the slavery question, and Turner boldly turned the tables on the Civil War–preoccupied historians of his day by explaining the end of slavery as a function of the frontier, in the person of the man Turner called the greatest westerner of all, Abe Lincoln of Illinois. The frontier thesis was the most popular during exactly the years when the Jim Crow system was the least contested, from the 1890s through the 1930s. The Turner thesis invited white northerners and white southerners to unite in thinking about America together, without being distracted by disagreements about black Americans. The most influential of the Jim Crow era's historians of slavery, Ulrich B. Phillips, who is now remembered for the overbearing racism of his account, was a doctoral advisee of Turner's. Yet the narrative of amalgamation visible in the writings of many historians of our own time[76] concentrates on the people and the relationships that Turner ignored, and on the behavioral and discursive answers Americans have offered to the question of ethnoracial mixture during the 110 years since he wrote.

These multiple answers, taken together, support the consensus of contemporary social science that the communities of descent sometimes called either racial or ethnic are highly contingent entities, with boundaries more subject to state power than was normally supposed by earlier generations, whose members were often blind to their own agency in creating and preserving these boundaries, taking as primordial the stuff of history that they themselves had helped to make. Yet nothing in American history calls into question the truism that boundaries are necessary, or that the maintenance of any solidarity requires exclusions as well as inclusions. And in an era of global dynamics, the challenge of drawing the "circle of the we" is more central than ever: where to try to draw what boundaries, with whom, and around what?[77]

This issue is now prominent on the agendas of many societies around the world, especially in European nations increasingly populated by immigrants from Asia, the Middle East, and the Caribbean. The history of the United States is potentially instructive in this contemporary setting not because this nation has drawn its social boundaries wisely or justly—far from it. It is beyond the scope of this essay to try to outline what the world might make of the American story of amalgamation and hypodescent. But I suspect that among the most important "lessons of American history," if that phrasing is not too strong, is one as humbling as it is hopeful: the history of the United States shows that even a nation carrying a heavy load of racism can incorporate individuals from an imposing variety of communities of descent on terms of considerable intimacy. The case of the United States implicitly refuses to let other nations off the hook that is presented to all immigrant-receiving democracies by the egalitarian ideals for which Western Europe has been so vital a cradle.

Among the Americans who have understood that European ideological heritage, especially as it came to the United States directly from England, was Herman Melville. He was also a fierce prophet of America's role as an agent of the further development, if not the perfection, of English liberty. The long-term world-historical mission of the United States was to "forever extinguish the prejudices of national dislikes," Melville proclaimed in 1849. This great contemporary of Wendell Phillips, Frederick Douglass, and Ralph Waldo Emerson envisaged a future in which the dispersed children of Adam and Eve would find each other in America, there to experience under the ordinance of democracy a Pentecostal moment. All the tribes of the earth will testify with cloven tongues of fire to their common humanity, yet the language in which they will speak, said Melville, will be "the language of Britain."[78] And so, in a manner and with many interruptions, and up to a point, it has been.

But we must distinguish between the empirically warranted narrative of amalgamation, punctuated as it is by hypodescent racialization, and the extravagance of the amalgamation fantasy. The latter is increasingly common in the public culture of the

United States today. We see it in journalistic accounts not only of the lives of Tiger Woods, Mariah Carey, and other mixed-descent celebrities but also of the cross-color marriages by leading politicians. Some commentators predict that ethnoracial distinctions in the United States will disappear in the twenty-first century. Perhaps they are right, but there is ample cause to doubt it. And a glance at the history of Brazil, where physical mixing even of blacks and whites has magnificently failed to achieve social justice and to eliminate a color hierarchy, should chasten those who expect too much from mixture alone. Moreover, inequalities by descent group are not the only kind of inequalities. In an epoch of diminished economic opportunities and of apparent hardening of class lines, the diminution of racism may leave many members of historically disadvantaged ethnoracial groups in deeply unequal relation to whites simply by virtue of class position. Even the end of racism at this point in history would not necessarily ensure a society of equals.

Fortunately, the distinction between the fantasy and the historical narrative is not hard to draw. Even Hollywood, in its best moments, can draw it. In *Bulworth*, a popular motion picture of 1998, forty years after Hannah Arendt's indiscretion, an indiscreet senator tells a national television audience that racism can be ended by wholesale intermarriage. "All we need," said Warren Beatty's Senator Bulworth, "is a voluntary, free-spirited, open-ended program of procreative racial deconstruction."[79] But the filmmakers shrewdly inserted these lines in a speech that the senator delivered while seized by a truth-telling dementia. So, we are to believe that there is a measure of truth to what he says, but you have to be crazy to say it. And that is where the United States enters the twenty-first century: wise enough to know how far it is from fulfilling Melville's prophecy but crazy enough to believe in it, at least part of the time.

2

The One Drop Rule and
the One Hate Rule

T his essay picks up from where "Amalgamation and Hypodescent" left off. Here, I explore more systematically the relationship between the hypodescent racialization of African Americans and the tendency of governmental and private agencies to treat non-black minorities according to the same rules established for black victims of white racism. I focus especially on the slowness of policy-makers and social critics to come to grips with the experience of Americans of Asian ancestry. I take the 1998 Clinton Commission's "Initiative on Race" as an example for this slowness. I argue that the more we understand the unique invidiousness of the "one drop rule" as applied to "blacks," the weaker the hold on us of the "one hate rule" according to which anti-discrimination remedies designed for black people are uncritically applied to non-black victims of white racism. And vice-versa. As the case for the one hate rule weakens, the unique racism of the one drop rule becomes all the more apparent. The rules have come to affect each other dialectically.

I argue, further, that what we learn from historians and social scientists about the conditions that promote the overrepresentation of some demographic groups in economic and educational elites (Jewish Americans, Japanese Americans, and South Asian Americans, for example) are relevant to our debates over the sources of the underrepresentation in the same social spaces of other demographic groups (including African Americans, Mexican Americans, and American Indians). Hence what I say here connects with Chapter Eight of this volume, "Rich, Powerful, and Smart: Jewish Overrepresenation Should Be Explained rather than Mystified or Avoided."

This essay grows out of a series of workshops convened by Kenneth Prewitt, the former Director of the United States Bureau of the Census, for the purpose of debating just what the questions about race, ethnicity, and nationality should look like in the federal censuses of the future. Accordingly, I express concern about a system that by default dumps on the Census Bureau the authority to decide which particular communities of descent belong to large groups called "races" and to decide, implicitly, which descent communities carry with their category presumptive eligibility for descent-defined benefits. Among the points at issue is exactly which social distinctions matter for the purposes of public policy in the United States, and why. If it is naïve and irresponsible to suppose that the United States is one big, undivided solidarity, in which ethnoracial distinctions do not affect the destiny of individuals, so, too, is it naïve and irresponsible to suppose that all victims of white racism are identically disabled and defined by that racism, no matter what their class position, their length of time in the United States, and what may have been the historical circumstances of their descent community prior to immigration.

This essay was published in Daedalus *(Winter 2005): 18–28.*

Two portentous practices within the public discussion of "race" in the United States since the late 1960s are rarely analyzed together. One is the method by which we decide which individuals are "black." The other is our habit of conflating the mistreatment of blacks with that of non-black minorities. Both practices compress a great range of phenomena into ostensibly manageable containers. Both function to keep the concept of race current amid mounting pressures that threaten to render it anachronistic. Both invite reassessment at the start of the twenty-first century.

The prevailing criterion for deciding who is black is of course the principle of hypodescent. This "one drop rule" has meant that anyone with a visually discernable trace of African, or what used to be called "Negro," ancestry is, simply, black. Comparativists have long noted the peculiar ordinance this mixture-denying principle has exercised over the history of the United States. Although it no longer has the legal status it held in many states during the Jim Crow era, this principle was reinforced in the civil rights era as a basis for anti-discrimination remedies. Today it remains in place as a formidable convention in many settings and dominates debates about the categories appropriate for the federal census. The movement for recognition of "mixed race" identity has made some headway, including for people with a fraction of African ancestry, but most governments, private agencies, educational institutions, and advocacy organizations that classify and count people by ethnoracial categories at all continue to perpetuate hypodescent racialization when they talk about African Americans.[1]

This practice makes the most sense when anti-discrimination remedies are in view. If discrimination has proceeded on the basis of the one drop rule, so too should anti-discrimination remedies. But even when anti-discrimination remedies are not at issue, most Americans of all colors think about African American identity in either/or terms: you are black, or you are not. It is common for people to say, "I'm half Irish and half Jewish" without one's listener translating the declaration into terms other than the speaker's. One can even boast, "I'm one-eighth Cherokee" without causing the listener to quarrel with that fraction or to doubt that the speaker is basically a white person. But those who say things like "I'm half Irish and half black" are generally understood *really* to be black, and "I'm one-eighth African American" is not part of the genealogical boasting that infuses American popular culture.

The second portentous practice is the treating of all victims of white racism alike, regardless of how differently this racism has affected African Americans, Latinos, Indians, and Asian Americans, to say nothing of the subdivisions within each of these communities of descent. When federal agencies developed affirmative action programs in the late 1960s, they identified Asian Americans, Hispanics, and Indians along with African Americans as eligible groups. As John Skrentny has shown, entitlements for non-black groups were predicated on the assumption that such groups were like blacks in their social experience.[2] Other disadvantaged groups, including women, impoverished Anglo whites, impoverished European ethnics, and gays and lesbians, were less successful in gaining entitlements during the so-called minority rights revolution because they were not perceived as victims of white racism. Yet the officials who designed entitlement programs for the purposes of remedying white racism often homogenized those descent groups colloquially coded as black, brown, red, and yellow. There was a good reason for this. White racism was real, had expressed itself against every one of these color-coded groups, and was a problem in American life that demanded correction.

The notion that all descent groups whose ancestry could be located outside Europe were like blacks, however, had not been prominent previously in the proclaimed self-conception of these non-black minority groups, nor in much of what public discussion there was of their history and circumstances. The histories of each of these communities were almost always presented to their own members as well as to the society at large in terms that took their differences into account, including the specific ways in which whites had abused them. These histories, moreover, were usually about particular descent groups, such as Chinese Americans or Mexican Americans, rather than about what came to be called "panethnic" groups, such as Asian Americans and Latinos.[3] Japanese Americans had been subject to property-owning restrictions and had been incarcerated without due process during World War II, and all but a few immigrants from Asia had been denied naturalization until 1952. Immigrants from Mexico had always been able to achieve citizenship and were not included in the miscegenation laws that prevented nonwhites from marrying whites, but these immigrants and their descendants had been subject to other abuses, including school segregation and exclusion from juries in many jurisdictions until courts eliminated these practices in the decade after World War II. Mexican Americans, moreover, despite their overwhelmingly immigrant origins, did come from a country that had lost territory to the United States, and sometimes defined themselves as a conquered people, like the Indians. The Indians themselves had their own story, featuring deaths on a horrendous scale through disease and genocide. But beyond emphasizing these and many other differences, spokespersons for these non-black groups sometimes partook of the anti-black racism of the white majority. As late as the early 1960s, for example, spokespersons for Mexican Americans in Los Angeles made a point of saying that their community wanted little to do with blacks in the same city.

Utterances of this latter kind diminished rapidly in the late 1960s as political alliances were forged between black advocacy organizations and organizations speaking for other descent groups. The idea that Asian Americans, Latinos, and Indians were indeed like blacks gained ground and was marked vividly with a designation especially popular in the 1980s: "people of color." The downplaying of the differences between non-black minorities and blacks was practiced first by officials and then by activists who came to understand that by applying "the black model" to their own group they had a better chance of getting the sympathetic attention of officials and courts. White racism thus ironically came to be assigned the same capacity traditionally assigned to one drop of black blood: *the capacity to define equally whatever it touched*, no matter how the affected entity was constituted and what its life circumstances might have been. We have been living by a principle of white racist hypovictimization: we can call it the one hate rule, with the understanding that the colloquial use of "hate" follows the language conventions of recent years, when we speak of "hate speech" and "hate crimes."

Both the one hate rule and the one drop rule have recently come under increasing pressure. But before I take up these pressures and suggest some of the potentially deep changes in

American race discourse they might produce, I want to clarify the historical circumstances that have endowed these rules with such force.

The property interests of slaveholders and the social priorities of Jim Crow racism are central to the principle of hypodescent. Keeping the color line sharp facilitated the enslavement of children begotten upon slave women by white men. The offspring of these couplings would grow up as slaves in a race-specific slave system. The principle was sharpened under Jim Crow, when opposition to social equality for blacks was well served by a monolithic notion of blackness accompanied by legislation that outlawed as miscegenation black-white marriages but that left less strictly regulated any non-marital sex in which white males might engage with black females. Some slave-era and Jim Crow governments did employ fractional classifications, providing distinctive rights and privileges for "octoroons," "quadroons," and "mulattoes," but this fractional approach was hard to administer, invited litigation, and blurred lines that many whites preferred to keep clear. "Mulatto" was dropped from the federal census after 1920, and more and more state governments went the way of Virginia, whose miscegenation statute as revised in 1924 classified as white only a person "who has no trace whatsoever of blood other than Caucasian."

The combination of these miscegenation laws with the principle of hypodescent consolidated and perpetuated the low-class positions of African Americans in much of the United States. By marking all offspring of white-black couplings as bastards, governments in many jurisdictions prevented these offspring from inheriting the property of a white father. Although the legendary Virginia statute, along with all other racial restrictions on marriage, was invalidated in 1967 by the U.S. Supreme Court in the case of *Loving v. Virginia,* the one drop rule classically formulated in the Virginia statute was not affected in its capacity as a convention operating throughout American society. Traditional white racism perpetuated this convention, but so, too, did the social solidarity of an African American community whose borders had been shaped by that racism. It is no wonder that the officials, courts, and advocacy organizations that designed and defended affirmative action measures showed no interest in mixture. Even if "light-skinned blacks" had sometimes experienced a less consistently brutal style of discrimination than that experienced by the darkest of African Americans, there was no doubt that any person perceived as having any black ancestry whatsoever was rightly included in the anti-discrimination remedies being developed in the late 1960s and early 1970s.

But what about non-black victims of white racism? Awareness of the reality of discrimination against non-blacks led to the conclusion that all ethnoracially defined victims of white racism might as well be made the beneficiaries of the same new set of entitlements being developed in the civil rights era, even in the absence of anyone's having lobbied for that result. (Indians, to be sure, were always subject to an additional, separate set of programs following from the distinctive constitutional status of Indian tribes.) When the Equal Employment Opportunity Commission (EEOC) designed its precedent-setting employer reporting form (EEO-1) in 1965, the EEOC included Indians, Asian Americans, and Latinos along with African Americans as the groups to be counted in relation to its mission. In fact, the EEOC was almost entirely concerned with African Americans: what percentage of those employable were actually employed in a given labor market? At the public hearing designed to collect reactions to this reporting form, no voice mentioned even in passing the situation of the non-black minorities.[4]

Virtually everyone in power at the time assumed the non-black minorities to be so tiny a part of the picture as to require no discussion and to entail no policy dilemmas for the future. Support for the Civil Rights Act of 1964 and for the specific mission and methods of the EEOC established under its terms was deeply informed by a popular understanding of the history of the victimization of African Americans in particular, and not by any comparably deep understanding of the acknowledged mistreatment of Latinos and Asian Americans. To call attention to this truth about the civil rights era is not to downplay the reality of white racism against non-blacks in American history right up to the time officials and courts acted. Rather, the point is that remedying the abuse of non-blacks was almost an afterthought to remedying anti-black racism.

Nothing illustrates this fact more dramatically than the lack of sustained public debate on the eligibility of immigrants and their offspring for affirmative action. This silence resulted partly because the Latino and Asian American populations were still small (about 4.5 percent and 1 percent, respectively, in the census of 1970), and because the Immigration and Nationality Act of 1965 that eventually transformed the ethnoracial demography of the United States, and revolutionized the meaning of ethnoracially defined entitlements, was not expected to significantly increase immigration from Latin America and Asia. Yet the numbers of Latin American and Asian immigrants mounted in the 1970s, yielding more and more non-black Americans who were not the descendants of those Chinese American, Japanese American, and Mexican American families that had been abused in the United States, and who were thus less analogous than were non-immigrant Latinos and Asian Americans to the descendants of enslaved Americans. Indeed, the number of new immigrants between 1970 and 2000 who were eligible for at least some affirmative action benefits came to about 26 million, the same number of eligible African Americans as measured by the census of 1980. More strikingly yet, many of the new immigrants and their children proved able, especially in the Asian American case, to make their way around racist barriers in education, business, and the workforce that continued to inhibit the progress of African Americans.

This emerging social reality might have triggered a rethinking of the one hate rule and stimulated a genuine effort to confront the distinctive history and needs of the several non-black groups on each group's own terms. But the system then in place created a huge disincentive for such a rethinking: the black model was working quite well. It helped get the attention of officials and courts, enabling them to recognize and understand the victimization of non-black minorities. As early as 1968, the Chicano youth activists in Los Angeles were declaring "Brown and Black" to be one and the same. As the most careful scholar of that episode has observed, writers in the Chicano movement's magazine *La Raza,* even while surrounded by older Mexican Americans whose group advocacy had been based on the affirmation of white identity, "asserted that Mexican identity, when measured in terms of history, geography, oppressions, and dreams, was functionally black."[5] Hence the one hate rule was quietly enacted by a variety of non-black advocacy groups as well as by officials and courts.

Neither the EEOC nor anyone else designing and approving affirmative action programs predicated on the ideal of proportional representation seems to have anticipated what could have happened if one or another of the designated groups came to be overrepresented instead of underrepresented. In the late 1960s and very early 1970s, there were very few Asian Americans, Latinos, and Indians in most of the same employment and educational spaces in which African Americans were underrepresented in relation to their percentage in the total population. Instead of inquiring into the specific causes of the underrepresentation of the various groups, one could assume with some justice that behind all cases was white racism of one degree or another. The one hate rule was good enough. At least for a while.

But as the numbers of Asian Americans increased dramatically through chain migrations in the 1970s and 1980s, and began to affect the public face of American society especially in California, a striking challenge to the one hate rule appeared. It became hard to overlook that Asian Americans, even if subject to discrimination as "foreign" and thus "not really American," were overrepresented rather than underrepresented in many universities and professions and among high-income householders. Well before the end of the 1980s, the Census Bureau reported that average family income for Asian Americans, even when the income for recently arrived immigrants from Southeast Asia was included, was higher than that for non-Hispanic whites. Asian Americans were quietly dropped from some private affirmative action programs (not from those operated by the federal government), but what public discussion there was of the success of Asian Americans was clouded by the problematic concept of "the model minority." The idea that African Americans, Latinos, and Indians had something wrong with them structurally—some genetic inferiority or deeply embedded cultural deficiency from which the wonderful Asians were free—was sometimes implied, and was of course vigorously contested.

Given the prior assumption that all ethnoracial minorities were more or less equally the victims of white racism, how could one talk about the success of Asian Americans without appearing to deny the power of white racism or to engage, however subtly, in a racist discourse against African Americans, Latinos, and Indians? That this pitfall could indeed be avoided was proved by a growing academic literature exploring with increasing rigor the different historical circumstances of the various American ethnoracial groups popularly called "minorities" or "people of color." That literature recognized, for example, the unique legacy of slavery and Jim Crow for African Americans, and assessed the pre-immigration social position and commercial experience for many Asian Americans.[6] Bengali engineers and Chihuahuan agricultural laborers really did bring different pre-immigration experiences and skills to the United States. Not innate "racial" characteristics, but empirically warrantable social conditions could illuminate the contrasting destinies of different descent communities in the

United States. Yet public policy discussions did not take much advantage of the invitation offered by Asian American success to rethink the one hate rule. Far from it.

A mark of the persistence of the one hate rule is its dominance of President Clinton's Initiative on Race, as displayed in *One America in the 21st Century: Forging a New Future*, the 1998 report of the Initiative's advisory board. Although the impeachment of Clinton distracted attention from this document at the time of its release, it is the only major president-sponsored assessment of race since the Kerner Commission's report of thirty years before. The very banality of *One America in the 21st Century* renders that document all the more revealing a depository of publicly acceptable "race talk" in the United States at the turn of the twenty-first century.

Central to that talk is the assertion that any differences between the particular varieties of "racial" discrimination and abuse are incidental to what those varieties have in common, and the assumption that the same set of policies can deal with virtually all those varieties of disadvantage. The advisory board does point (with a series of "signposts of historical episodes," which they distinguish from the "comprehensive" history they disclaim) to a handful of particular experiences: the conquest of the Indians, the enslavement and segregation of black people, "the conquest and legal oppression of Mexican American and other Hispanics," the "forced labor of Chinese Americans," and the "internment of Japanese Americans." Even "new immigrants" from Southeast Asia "continue to feel the legacy of discriminatory laws against Asian Pacific Americans because they continue to be perceived and treated as foreigners." In keeping with this last observation, which incorporates the most recent of voluntary immigrants into the same frame with the descendants of slaves and of the conquered and ruthlessly slaughtered indigenous population, the advisory board offers the following summary of the salient history: "Each of the minority groups discussed above share in common a history of legally mandated and socially and economically imposed subordination to white European Americans and their descendants."[7]

This perspective informs the entire document, especially the advisory board's recommendations. All but five of the more than fifty recommendations are general to all victims of racism. Four of the five exceptions deal with the special problems of Indians and Alaskan natives, and the fifth calls for better data-gathering on non-black minority groups. Not a single one of the advisory board's recommendations speaks to the specific claims of African Americans on the national conscience. Yet blacks, and blacks alone, inherit a multi-century legacy of group-specific enslavement and hypodescent racialization long carried out under constitutional authority in the United States.

The contrast between the Asian American experience in recent years and the African American experience during the same period is systematically deemphasized by *One America in the 21st Century*. Only in a footnote and in one easily missed chart does the advisory board acknowledge that by the end of the 1980s Asian Americans had achieved an average annual family income higher even than that of non-Hispanic whites, and almost twice that of blacks and Hispanics. Repeatedly, the advisory board tries to shoehorn the Asian American experience into the space prescribed for it by the one hate rule. In a single sentence, the advisory board praises law enforcement agencies for investigating both the decapitation of a black man in Texas and the death threats to sixty Asian American students at a campus in California. A statement in the text to the effect that "criminal victimization rates are significantly greater for minorities and people of color than for whites, especially with regard to violent crime," makes no distinctions between the groups. But if one turns to the footnote documenting this statement, one learns that while the homicide rate is 58 per 100,000 for African Americans and 25 per 100,000 for Hispanics, it is only 8 per 100,000 for Asian Americans, which is close to the 5 per 100,000 for whites. Thus the proximity of Asian

Americans to non-Hispanic whites in one statistical sector after another is downplayed, ignored, or concealed. Many of the charts in the report that show inequality by ethnoracial group omit Asian Americans altogether. This is true of charts showing rates of college enrollment, median weekly earnings of male workers, and employment—all of which contrast whites to blacks and Hispanics. The advisory board is understandably determined to refute the myth that "the problem of racial intolerance in this country has been solved," but in its reluctance to particularize and measure the dimensions of this problem and to deal directly with the reasons why some Americans mistakenly believe the problem to be solved, it ends up weakening its case.[8] Asian American success in overcoming the worst consequences of white racism is the elephant in the advisory board's room.

At stake is the more precise location of the barriers that inhibit Americans of various communities of descent from participating more fully in the life of the nation. The more confident we can be about the social location of those barriers, the more likely we are as a nation to develop policies that target remedy to wrong in the effort to achieve a more equal society. If economic and social conditions antecedent to immigration are significant factors in explaining the relative success many Asian American groups have achieved, that suggests that white racism does not always have the same effect on everything it touches, but rather affects those objects differently depending on how those objects are constituted.

Even *One America in the 21st Century* approaches this insight when it distinguishes between the different destinies of Asian American groups, noting in a footnote that while 88 percent of Japanese Americans between the ages of twenty-five and twenty-nine have a high school diploma, only 31 percent of Hmong Americans do.[9] How recent the immigration and how strong or weak the class position of the group prior to immigration clearly make an enormous difference. This is true not only for Asian Americans but also for Hispanics. For instance, sociologists have explained repeatedly that recent illegal immigrants from Mexico encounter the United States and its white racism differently than do Cuban Americans whose families have been in the country for several decades, or than do descendants of earlier generations of migrants from Mexico who have more opportunities to learn English and to take advantage of whatever educational opportunities are at hand.

So great is the variety of experience among Hispanics that the Census Bureau would do well to think carefully about the basis for continuing to treat Hispanics as a single category at all. The census might drop this quasi-racial category and count instead those inhabitants who identify with descent communities from Mexico, Cuba, Puerto Rico, the Dominican Republic, Haiti, and other such defining points of origin. Instead of counting "Asians," the census might count people who trace their descent to China, Japan, Korea, Vietnam, India, Iran, the Philippines, Pakistan, Lebanon, Turkey, etc. Any public or private agency that wished for any reason—including the design and implementation of anti-discrimination remedies—to treat all Hispanics or Asians as a single group could easily reaggregate the groups counted separately by the census. Or a given agency might conclude, on the basis of what it learns about the social and economic circumstances of particular descent communities, and on the basis of its analysis of where responsibility for a given case of disadvantage lies, that some groups need affirmative action and others do not. Breaking down Hispanic into the actual descent groups that exist in the United States would facilitate this. So, too, with Americans of Asian descent. Neither Hispanics nor Asian Americans have an experience as unified as that of African Americans, and the Census Bureau needs a better justification than it has offered until now for the use of these panethnic, "racial" categories. By rejecting racial and quasi-racial categories, the census can liberate itself from de facto responsibility for deciding who is eligible for this or that program.[10]

Analysis of different segments of the black population, too, yields more precise information about the location of the barriers to full participation in American life. Black immigrants from the Caribbean and their descendants are more likely than the American-born heirs of the Jim Crow system to advance in education and employment and to marry outside their natal community. So too are black immigrants from Africa, as the public has recently been reminded by the remarkable career of Illinois politician Barack Obama, elected to the U.S. Senate in 2004.[11] Moreover, Dalton Conley has found that when blacks and whites with the same property holdings (as opposed merely to the same income, which is a less substantial indicator of economic position) are compared, the gap between black and white performance on Graduate Record Examinations and in several other arenas of achievement diminish to a point of statistical insignificance.[12] Class position, when accurately measured, makes a formidable difference. What our social science is telling us today is not that white racism has disappeared, nor even that it is unimportant, but that it interacts with a variety of other realities to create the patterns of inequality that social policy must address.

It is in the context of these social scientific findings that the status of "underrepresented minorities" invites reexamination with an eye toward better understanding those patterns of inequality. When the ideal of proportional representation entered affirmative action directives and jurisprudence in about 1970, a major objective was to get beyond "intentional" discrimination in order to confront prior, structural conditions producing inequality. But by promoting the idea that the mere fact of underrepresentation constituted evidence of discrimination, however indirect, officials and courts deflected attention from any and all possible specific explanations for why a particular descent group might be underrepresented in a particular employment or educational sector. What was lost in the process was an ability to deal forthrightly with the appearance of Asian Americans as an overrepresented minority.

Underrepresentation and overrepresentation constitute a logical syndrome. Should we not expect the same principles of causation to apply to both sides of the phenomenon? Might what we learn about the overrepresentation of particular descent groups—Korean Americans and Jewish Americans, for example—help us to understand the underrepresentation of others, and vice versa? This might seem obvious, but the analysis of overrepresentation, and of the historical processes by which ethnoracial groups that were once underrepresented have become overrepresented, usually stops with the white color line. The Irish, the Italians, the Poles, and the Jews, we say, became white. But invoking whiteness does not carry us very far. Appalachian whites are not overrepresented in the medical profession and in the nation's great universities, and some "people of color"—Chinese Americans and South Asian Americans, for example—are.

Jewish experience since 1945 is the most dramatic single case in all American history of a stigmatized descent group that had been systematically discriminated against under the protection of the law suddenly becoming overrepresented many times over in social spaces where its progress had been previously inhibited. The experience since 1970 of several Asian American groups is a second such dramatic case. These cases of success invite emphasis and explanation in relation to explanations for the social destiny of other descent-defined groups. What explains the overrepresentation of Jewish Americans, South Asian Americans, and Japanese Americans in the domains of American life where African Americans and Latinos are underrepresented? The failure to pursue this question implicitly strengthens largely unexpressed speculations that Jews and Asians are, after all, superior genetically to African Americans, Latinos, and American Indians—the groups whose underrepresentation is constantly at issue.

Yet the grounds for avoiding talk about the overrepresentation of Jewish Americans and some groups of Asian Americans diminish, if not disappear, once the relevant statistics are explained by taking full account of the conditions under which the various descent communities have been shaped.[13] Avoiding the forthright historical and social-scientific study of the question perpetuates the mystification of descent communities and subtly fuels the idea that the question's answer is really biological, and if made public will serve to reinforce invidious distinctions between descent groups. The open discussion of overrepresentation will not be racist if it proceeds on non-racist assumptions. We will not understand patterns of inequality in the United States until overrepresentation and underrepresentation are studied together and with the same methods. The one hate rule is an obstacle to such inquiries. But if the overrepresentation of African American males in prisons can be explained, as it often is, with reference to slavery, Jim Crow, and the larger history of the institutionalized debasement of black people, so, too, can the overrepresentation of Jewish Americans and Korean Americans in other social spaces be explained by historical conditions.

So the one hate rule, however sensible it may have seemed when informally adopted in the 1960s and 1970s, is increasingly difficult to defend. And the less blinded we are by it the more able we are to see the unique invidiousness of the one drop rule, its ironic twin. The practice of hypodescent racialization has entailed an absolute denial of the reality of extensive white-black mixing. It has embodied a total rejection of blackness and it has implied a deep revulsion on the part of empowered whites. This variety of white racism was cast into bold relief in the 1980s and 1990s by the dramatic upsurge of immigration from Latin America and Asia. The first of these immigrations displayed from the start an acknowledged and often celebrated mixture of European and indigenous ancestry, and produced children who married Anglos at a rising rate and who were not subject to hypodescent racialization as

Latinos. The new immigrants from Asia married Anglos at a considerably higher rate than Latinos did, and their offspring were not socially coerced to identify as 100 percent Asian.

Only a few years earlier, when affirmative action and the allied initiatives that eventually came to be called "multiculturalism" got started, the assumption had been that all the standard minority groups were clearly bounded, durable entities, kept in place by the power of white racism and by the internal adhesives of their communities of descent. But the experience of non-black minorities was sufficiently different from that of African Americans that the hypodescent racialization of the latter came to be more widely recognized as an index of the unique severity of anti-black racism in the United States. No wonder some frustrated African American activists campaigned for group-specific reparations. Hence the weakening of the one hate rule and the development of a critical perspective on the one drop rule proceeded dialectically. The more fully we understand the unique invidiousness of the principle of hypodescent as applied to "blacks," the weaker the hold of the one hate rule; and the weaker the hold of the one hate rule, the more able we are to confront at long last the exceptionally racist character of the one drop rule.[14]

3

The Historian's Use of
the United States and Vice Versa

*H*istorians specializing in the study of the United States are often scolded for speaking only to one another, creating a vacuum filled by journalists and ideologues less qualified than professional historians to explain to the American public the history of their own country. At the same time, these historians are often scolded for their persistent and insufficiently acknowledged nationalism, for their provincial failure to interpret the history of the United States in a cosmopolitan, global perspective. The two criticisms of scholarly practice pull historians in different directions. The more conscientiously a historian formulates in global terms the issues around which the study of American history revolves, the more removed he or she can become from the concerns of the public as measured by that public's enthusiasm for patriotic biographies of Great Americans. The more conscientiously a scholar writes with an eye on the "wider audience" publishers constantly and invidiously contrast to "a merely scholarly readership," the more removed he or she can become from the global dynamics with which intellectuals of our "post-national" era are increasingly and passionately engaged.*

This essay assesses the potentially conflicting claims on historians of the national solidarity of the United States and of the professional solidarity of the global community of scholars. It was commissioned by Thomas Bender of

57

New York University, the leader of a multi-year series of symposia on what the history of the United States would look like if studied with the full scope of world history in mind. I argue, against some of my fellow symposiasts, that the study of the United States as a nation is far from anachronistic because the national solidarity of the United States remains a historical agent of enormous power and consequence.

Although I wrote this prior to the unfolding of international politics in the wake of the attacks of September 11, 2001, I now take this essay's cautions against the abandonment of national history to be all the more pertinent. The actions of the United States in Iraq and elsewhere, and the American government's general disregard of international opinion, should remind us that the United States is a more formidable actor in history than ever. Yet the same course of events, and the willingness of so much of the American public to accept the unilateralism of their government, underscores the need of the public for exactly the global perspective that professional historians are equipped to provide.

This essay first appeared in Thomas Bender, ed., Rethinking American History in a Global Age *(Berkeley: University of California Press, 2002), 381–95.*

Nations can easily turn historians into tools. When David Potter etched this point into the collective mind of historians in 1962, he assumed that nations, for better or for worse, would remain the central subject of historians. Potter paused at the start of "The Historian's Use of Nationalism and Vice Versa" to find it a bit odd that he and his colleagues could really suppose that "the 2,500,000,000 people of the world would fall naturally into a series of national groups." But he went on swiftly and confidently to conclude that nations were *it.* That even a historian as skeptical as Potter could do this reveals the width of the gap between his historiographical era and ours.[1] Some four decades later, we routinely take the view that nations are only one of many central subjects. We have extensive subnational and transnational monographic literatures. We are preoccupied with the contingent, constructed character of nations. We are awash in "postnational" speculation that nation-states are on their way out. Furthermore, we easily understand a growing suspicion of nation-centered history as anachronistic at best and reactionary at worst. And we are more convinced than ever of the wisdom of Potter's caution against our being "used" by nations, even as we decide when and when not to apply the label "nation" to a given solidarity.

What are the prospects for national narrative today in the case of the United States? Where do historians of this particular nation now stand in relation to Potter's dilemma?

One obvious course of action is to focus less on the nation and more on its constituent parts, and on the transnational networks of which any nation is a node. With regard to the United States, we might argue, in Potter's terms, that in view of our sharp awareness of transnational and subnational experience, historians have less use for the United States than they once did. And the less use historians have for the United States, the less danger there is, presumably, that the United States will "use" historians. Hence an attractive escape from Potter's dilemma is to escape the nation, to "rescue history from the nation," as Prasenjit Duara has phrased this program in relation to the historiography of modern China.[2]

Yet nations are not the only formations that threaten to turn historians into tools. Nonnational and antinational movements and solidarities can do the same. In dealing with them, we may find ourselves without even the modest measure of control over our own instrumentality that we gain from our increasingly acute suspicion of the nation. By virtue of their presumed innocence, nonnational solidarities may be able to use us more easily than nations can. Potter specified for nations what is actually a generic problem for the historian in relation to any solidarity that holds moral resonance for historians or for their audiences.

The solidarities we call nations do, moreover, retain a justified hold on a substantial amount of our attention. Even if we accept Charles Maier's formulation of the 1970s as the end of a distinctive historical epoch of nation-centered human striving, it will not do to project onto the past the particular dispersion of power that Maier and others see as characteristic of the last quarter of the twentieth century.[3] Even should it be determined that the national community of the United States figures smaller in the lives of many of its citizens and inhabitants than it once did, that determination would provide no basis for a less nation-centered history of the United States during the years prior to this putative transformation. However likely or desirable we may judge a more transnational or postnational future to be, the national past remains no less formidable. Hence contemporary speculation about the replacement of the world of nations by a world of something-elses is of heuristic value at best to historians concerned with the people who have lived in the United States.

If there is any one nation in the contemporary world the history of which, *as a nation*, requires telling now, it is the one that displays the most successful nationalist project in all of modern history.[4] Despite the failure of some history faculties around the world to register this insight, the United States is of world-historical significance. What marks the national project of the United States as "successful" is not its virtue—although it would be disingenuous of me to deny that I personally believe that the United States does have many virtues—but certain simple, un-contested facts. Two-and-one-quarter centuries after its founding and 135 years after its Civil War, the United States is the most powerful nation-state in the world and the only twenty-first century power that operates under a constitution written in the eighteenth century. Its significance is measured by its sheer longevity, its influence in the world arena, and its absorption of a variety of peoples through immigration, conquest, and enslavement and emancipation. The formidable presence of the United States in the world has been achieved at notorious costs, including, as we historians have become quite skilled at demonstrating, the systematic mistreatment of people on the basis of color, language, and religion. One may lament the success of the United States, or at least the evils by which that success has been achieved. One may instead rejoice in what support the United States provides for whatever ideals one may hold. Or, one may be morally indifferent to it. And one can explain it in a number of different ways. But no matter how one judges the national project of the United States morally, and now matter how one explains it historically, the national project of the United States is part of the primal stuff of history to be engaged.

Thus historians do still have real use for the United States. And vice versa: the United States can no doubt use historians, and in ways that threaten their autonomy and their loyalty to the truth. Potter's dilemma persists.

But this dilemma now presents itself in a specific historiographical context that invites clarification. Among the winds of doctrine that have swept through the ranks of professional historians of the United States during the 1990s, two have been especially bracing. One pushes historians to speak to a nonprofessional public. The other pushes historians to interpret American history in truly global perspective. The first promises to affect the terms on which the United States might turn historians into tools. The second promises to affect the terms on which historians might achieve maximum independence.

Historians should work harder at being public intellectuals, we are told. Historians within the orbit of the Organization of American Historians are constantly calling upon one another to stop talking simply to ourselves. Rather, we should, in this popular version of our calling, write more "cross-over" books, engage more fully with the teaching of history in secondary and even elementary schools, coordinate our activities as research scholars with those of museum curators and public historians, challenge the sometimes benighted priorities of the History Channel, and generally integrate our work as historians more fully with our responsibilities to the public, above all, the public of the United States. These concerns have generated a multitude of initiatives, including closer official connections with public historians and the participation of academic historians in the National History Standards.

Yet historians are also told to stop thinking about the United States in the parochial terms of American citizenship. Historians encourage one another to adopt a global perspective on what goes on within the United States. Many of the same historians who support the OAH's outreach to the American public also support the "internationalization" of the field. In this internationalist view, we are to see the functions of the American national solidarity in the sweep of *Weltgeschichte*, and write history framed by the human species, and even with the earth itself in mind. Our history will be a lot better, we tell ourselves, if we liberate ourselves from a preoccupation with the role our work plays in the public life of the United States. This move toward the global is substantially strengthened by the surveillance of U.S.-based historians by a world community of historians finally taking a more active interest in U.S. history. After all, the particularistic tendencies and patriotic biases of German historians of German history, of Italian historians of Italian history, and of Japanese historians of Japanese history have all been scrutinized and significantly corrected by an international community of historians, in which leading roles have been played by U.S.-based specialists in the histories of those other nations. Are not historians within Germany, Italy, Japan, and a number of other nations less thoroughly "used" by their nations as a result of an international community of historians? Is it not an enormous boon to more fully warranted interpretations of the history of the United States, then, to have a genuinely international scholarly community engaged with the study of that history? The strength of this international community makes it less likely that the United States will turn historians into mere instruments. This incorporation of U.S.-based historians of the United States into a genuinely global community of scholars may help emancipate "American history," at long last, from its role as a historical theology for the civil religion of the United States.

But what then of the responsibilities of historians to a public smaller than the species? If the arguments for a global perspective are so compelling, what becomes of the distinctly American public to which we try to speak? Where does the intensified professionalism of a more global historiography meet the intensified obligation to get beyond professionalism to engage the civic culture of one's nation? Should historians determined to interpret the United States in global perspective renounce altogether any engagement with the destiny of that nation's political community? Should U.S.-based historians of the United States orient themselves to the American public any differently than Australian-, Brazilian-, French-, or Russian-based historians of the United States, and if so, on the basis of what theory? Is the record of historians who have sought to build, sustain, or diminish national consciousness in the United States so negative in all its variations that the whole enterprise of solidarity building and critical revision should be left to nonhistorians? To what extent does the mere act of writing national narrative implicate a historian in the national project, regardless of his or her intentions?

To make these questions explicit and to call attention to their importance is more to my purpose here than providing a series of convincing answers. A book published in the year 2001 entitled *Rethinking American History in a Global Age* might well end with this list of questions.

But I do want to engage Potter's dilemma in the context of these questions. Within globally oriented scholarship, I believe, there is still substantial room for national narrative that speaks to the American public, and that even has among its several purposes the critical maintenance of the United States considered as a political solidarity. In so arguing, I take collegial issue with a widely discussed essay on some of these questions, David Thelen's "Making History and Making the United States." Thelen and I are allies in the movements for internationalization and for greater public engagement by historians. Yet this particular essay of 1998 invites a critical response here for several reasons. It displays the very difficulty my reading of Potter warns against: in focusing so much on the dangers of the nation, we risk falling into the uncritical embrace of something else: in Thelen's case, formations that are not national and not professional. The piece was published in a European venue that is especially vital in the internationalization of the study of the history of the United States, the *Journal of American Studies.* "Making History and Making the United States" deals more systematically with the relevant issues than do Thelen's other, more episodic writings, some of which are closer to my own views. I cite some of these below by way of indicating the common ground within which my disagreements with Thelen are situated.

The critique of nation-centered scholarship Thelen offers in "Making History and Making the United States" concentrates heavily on the *motives* of historians over the course of two centuries. Of special concern are the "professionals" of the late nineteenth century who, like the businessmen of that epoch, were eager "to create and control national markets." Thelen reminds us that nationally minded historians have been actors in the process by which the people of the United States have come to think of themselves as a nation and have achieved a certain measure of loyalty to national political institutions.[5] But even if one were to accept without caveat Thelen's account of the motives of historians of the past, it does not follow that today's historians who place a priority on national history are of a political piece with those of fifty, a hundred, or a hundred and fifty years ago. Thelen leaves the impression that these scholars of our own time are uncritical inheritors and perpetuators of a narrow nationalistic tradition.

In fact, to study the nation is not necessarily to be an ideological nationalist. National narrative is now being practiced with great skill by a host of contemporaries who can be construed as American nationalists only if our understanding of "nationalist" is considerably more commodious than that assumed by Thelen's account of our historiographical ancestors. Eric Foner's *The Story of*

American Freedom is a widely appreciated example.[6] Linda Kerber's *The Constitutional Right to Be Ladies: Women and the Obligations of Citizenship* should serve as a reminder of the importance of constitutional history, and of the role of state power in affecting the lives of individuals.[7] Another prize-winning volume that resoundingly vindicates national narrative is Rogers Smith's *Civic Ideals: Conflicting Visions of Citizenship in U.S. History,* which shows, in Smith's words, how "lawmakers pervasively and unapologetically structured U.S. citizenship in terms of illiberal and undemocratic racial, ethnic, and gender hierarchies, for reasons rooted in basic, enduring imperatives of political life."[8] The *Oxford History of the United States*, perhaps our era's most conspicuous endeavor in the production of national narrative, now includes distinguished volumes by Robert Middlekauff, James McPherson, David Kennedy, and James Patterson.[9] If Thelen wishes to find fault with the motives of nation-centered historians, let him address these contemporaries.

Thelen's critique of nation-centered history is caught up in a larger complaint. He finds professional historians insufficiently responsive to public taste. Thelen urges scholars to spend less time talking about the nation and more time talking about "the ways that individuals make and remake their larger circumstances and cultures and institutions." He reminds us that many people consider "the past of their own families to be more important than the past of the nation." Largely on the basis of evidence that the public believes this, he calls for "a new kind of history" focusing more on individuals and their families. This new history would be "one in which people can be participants, not spectators, and can use the past to explore their agency as human beings." Thelen complains that historians, by "focusing on conflicts and changes in the larger circumstances, institutions, and cultures," tend to "emphasize that individuals and families are shaped by these larger categories—which are largely about power."[10]

Well, historians do tend to make a lot of power. And for good reason. Historians have traditionally felt a responsibility to tell the truth about the dispersion and consequences of power. Looking away from the nation, and toward subnational and transnational aspects of the experience of inhabitants of the United States, may entail a withdrawal from this responsibility. Power turns out to be real concern of Thelen's, but more by way of influencing its future deployment than by clarifying its past structure and operation. A design of his program for a less nation-centered history is the empowering of some people and the disempowering of other people. "Interrogating nation-centeredness leads to interrogation of the authority of those who have promoted national perspectives," he tells us in relation to an extended commentary on nationalist sentiments in the development of American historiography from David Ramsey to today's "liberal nationalists."

Thelen wants to make nonhistorians into active "participants" in the writing of history and to emphasize their own "agency" in the history that gets written.[11] Noble as this apparently democratic and egalitarian aspiration may be, the aspiration invokes and begs questions about agency that historians routinely ask. Debates over what role individuals and groups and inherited structures and contingent conditions play in determining a given outcome are standard business for historians. Social historians have for a number of decades now been exploring the agency of subnational and transnational elements of American society. Biography, too, is a well-established mode of historical study. Indeed, attention to social groups and families and individuals reached a point of such saturation in history and the social sciences generally by the end of the 1980s that a chorus of voices asked to "bring the state back in."

Thelen implies that focusing on the agency of individuals and families is a good thing for historians to do regardless of just how much or how little force such agency might be shown to have in any given situation. He is much affected by the feelings of the public as revealed in "a random telephone survey of 1,400 Americans" that Thelen and a colleague conducted in 1994. Thelen here justifies the historiographical diminution of the American nation largely on the grounds that this diminution will provide a more user-friendly history to those parts of the public whose talk about history Thelen describes sympathetically in the following account of his interviewees:

> They talked about needs, ambitions, dreams, love, and fears, and they reflected on the past to learn about how to treat other individuals and how to make a difference in the course of their lives. They used terms like pride, shame, guilt, commitment, and trust. Their narratives were about aspiration, tragedy, and irony that have often been better presented by poets and novelists than historians because they are about human dilemmas that transcend time and place.[12]

This gushing appreciation for the language of everyperson invites a suspicion that historians will become tools of untutored public opinion. Popular memory and critical history have their own claims, as Michael Kammen and Kerwin Klein have argued convincingly.[13] If Robert Paxton had been respectful of popular memory in France, and of the stories each family wanted to tell of its heroic role in the resistance to Nazism, the world would be considerably less cognizant than it now is of French participation in the destruction of France's own Jewish population under the Vichy regime. The story people wanted to hear was one of dogged subversion of Nazism. Paxton's defiance of those desires was crucial to his now acclaimed achievement.[14] It would never do, of course, to suppose that only professional historians have the ability to see evil and the courage to address it, nor would it do even to suppose that most history writing by professionals is distinguished by these virtues. But studies of World War II provide an excellent example of how the obligations of professional integrity can conflict with the pressures to give the public the kind of history it wants.

Most of the people Thelen and his colleague, Roy Rosenzweig interviewed described the history they had studied in school as "boring," and this Thelen hopes to change. But a national history more skillfully conceived and executed might well be as relevant to this goal as might a history less national in scope. National history sometimes does include events that involve ambitions, fears, pride, shame, and tragedy, and indeed all of the generic human experiences Thelen lists. The exceedingly popular, nationally oriented books of Stephen Ambrose and David McCullough certainly display these generic aspects of human striving, as do the frequent presentations these two historians make on television. Many of the programs on cable TV's History Channel, a mainstay of national narrative, present the American past in terms that exactly fit the sensibility Thelen attributes to an American public poorly served by academic historians.

But one need not look beyond academic historical writing to find prominent examples of national history that include the generic experiences that most interest the public, and that meet the most demanding of professional standards. One compelling recent instance is David M. Kennedy's *Freedom from Fear: The American People in Depression and War, 1929–1945*, which deserves attention here because it is located on the historiographical spectrum about as far away as it is possible to get from the historiographical future envisaged by "Making History and Making the United States." Kennedy's contribution to the *Oxford History of the United States* is largely about presidents and generals. *Freedom from Fear* concentrates on affairs of state and on aspects of society, culture, and economy that impinge on how those affairs are resolved. This book also shows that a global perspective and a national narrative are not incompatible. The point is to determine when and how to bring the subnational and supranational histories into the national narrative. And this conception of the challenge, let me hasten to point out, is largely accepted by Thelen himself in some of his more recent writing in the *Journal of American History*.[15]

Kennedy's accounts of the suffering experienced during the Depression and of the horrors experienced in warfare convey a sense that every life counted, but he never implies that each exercised equal influence over the course of events. He reminds us of the sergeant who improvised the "hedgehog" that enabled tanks to better penetrate the defenses of Normandy, but he has the good sense to do so in a footnote. Kennedy does not allow his readers the fantasy that the representation of the personal experience of soldiers can be a substitute for analysis of the course of a military engagement. One can appreciate what both an excellent commercial film like *The Thin Red Line* and a scholarly book like *Freedom from Fear* tell us about Guadalcanal without expecting either to perform the tasks of the other. The relative agency of Franklin Roosevelt and Douglas McArthur and the other principals amid the webs of circumstance and the contingencies of experience is a major theme of *Freedom from Fear.*

But no feature of Kennedy's treatment of *The American People in Depression and War* is more relevant to developing a perspective alternative to Thelen's than is Kennedy's studied refusal to yield to public memory. His account of World War II is written against a popular narrative of a "good" and "just" war "waged by a peaceful people aroused by anger only after intolerable provocation, a war stoically endured by those and home and fought in faraway places by brave and wholesome young men and dedicated women standing behind them on the production lines." Kennedy's own narrative challenges the reading public to confront what historians know better than the public does. Kennedy's own summary paragraph is worth quoting here, despite its length, because it so cogently brings together themes of this book that mark it as a synthesis of a generation of professional scholarship, and displays a global perspective that Kennedy shows can inform a distinctly national story. National narrative informed by transnational values and embedded in a world-historical perspective is indeed possible, and in an idiom popular enough to win, as Kennedy's book now has, a Pulitzer Prize. In the passage I quote, Kennedy, without denying the aspects of the war that the public remembers as good and just, is describing aspects of the war that the American people largely ignored or suppressed, but that they might have reflected upon in 1945 had they truly understood their situation and possessed the moral courage to face it:

> They might have reflected with some discomfort on how slowly they had awakened to the menace of Hitlerism in the isolationist 1930s; on how callously they had barred the door to those seeking to flee from Hitler's Europe; on how heedlessly they had provoked Japan into a probably avoidable war in a region where few American interests were at stake; on how they had largely fought with America's money and machines and with Russia's men, had fought in Europe only late in the day, against a foe mortally weakened by three years of brutal warfare in the east, had fought in the Pacific with a bestiality they did not care to admit; on how they had profaned their constitution by interning tens of thousands of citizens largely because of their race; on how they had denied most black Americans a chance to fight for their country; on how they had sullied their nation's moral standards with terror bombing in the closing months of the war; on how their leaders' stubborn insistence on unconditional surrender had led to the incineration of hundreds of thousands of already defeated Japanese, first by fire raids, then by nuclear blast; on how poorly Franklin Roosevelt had prepared for the postwar era, how foolishly he had banked on goodwill and personal charm to compose the conflicting interests of nations, how little he had taken his countrymen into his confidence, even misled them, about the nature of the peace that was to come; on how they had abandoned the reforming agenda of the New Deal years to chase in wartime after the sirens of consumerism; on how they alone among warring peoples had prospered, emerging unscathed at home while 405,339 American soldiers, sailors, marines, and airmen had died. These men were dignified in death by their service, but they represented proportionately fewer military casualties than in any other major belligerent country. Beyond the war's dead and wounded and their families, few Americans had been touched by the staggering sacrifices and unspeakable anguish that the war had visited upon millions of other people around the globe.[16]

Freedom from Fear is an imposing, enthralling work of national history even though it does not cover everything of historical significance that took place within, or surrounding, the United States between 1929 and 1945. It contains next to no intellectual history, very little religious history, and not much about the arts, popular or elite. Reinhold Niebuhr is not mentioned; nor is Margaret Mead, William Faulkner, or Benny Goodman.

Even within Kennedy's justifiable focus on affairs of state, one can imagine a yet more international focus. Daniel T. Rodgers's *Atlantic Crossings: Social Politics in a Progressive Age* convincingly details a transatlantic intellectual and organization matrix that informed the making of government domestic policy through the 1930s. It was the war, indeed, that sharply diminished this international policy discourse just as, paradoxically, the United States became more politically involved beyond its borders: having supposed that they had "saved the world," Rodgers remarks of Americans of the 1940s, they had trouble imagining that they still had "much to learn from it."[17] But if only Rodgers's Americans had understood the war and the world of 1945 the way Kennedy now reconstructs them, Americans might not have been so arrogant, and so unwilling to continue to learn from the western European tradition of social democracy.

That tradition is among the chief subjects of another book that deserves attention in any consideration of fate and promise of nation-centered history. In *Uncertain Victory: Social Democracy and Progressivism in European and American Thought, 1870–1920,* James T. Kloppenberg challenges American exceptionalist assumptions with regard to pragmatism and progressivism, while taking careful account of the distinctive contexts of the four national cultures in which his cast of characters developed their ideas. This 1986 book interprets as closely related—and indeed as structurally connected—many of the chief developments in modern philosophy and political argumentation in four nations of the North

Atlantic West, France, Germany, the United Kingdom, and the United States.[18] *Uncertain Victory* can serve to remind us that transnational history is being vigorously researched and written in terms that complement and enrich, rather than necessarily undermine, national narratives.

Intellectual history, the subfield to which Kloppenberg's widely appreciated book was contributed, would seem to be an ideal place to look for alternatives to an excessively nation-focused scholarship. Intellectual historians have long been attentive to what Thelen describes in passing as the "transnational circulations" of "religion or art or ideas" that parallel the "story of how capitalism and its agents" cross "national borders."[19] Thelen might have turned, for example, to several prominent books of the decade of the 1970s that addressed American thought in the context of exactly such transnational circulations, among them Henry F. May's *The Enlightenment in America,* Bruce Kuklick's *The Rise of American Philosophy,* Daniel W. Howe's collection on *Victorian America,* and James R. Moore's *The Post-Darwinian Controversies.*[20] While social historians of that decade made their greatest contributions by exploring a variety of local settings within the United States, creating a substantial "subnational" historiography of groups within American society, intellectual historians were practicing an increasingly transnational scholarship.

There are other, equally obvious fields in which to look for strong international emphases. Historians of diplomacy and historians of religion have long maintained an international frame of reference. Most surprising of all, Thelen does not turn to historians of science, perhaps the supreme exemplars of the study of things American in the specific contexts of international communities. The ways in which the international endeavor of science takes particular forms within particular national cultures has been a concern of historians of science for a full century, ever since the publication in 1904 of J. T. Merz's classic discussion of national styles of science in the first volume of his *A History of European Thought in the Nineteenth Century*.[21]

What might a nation-centered scholarship that speaks both to a global community of professional historians and to citizens of the United States look like? The examples I have provided above, especially Kennedy's *Freedom from Fear*, may be a sufficient answer to this question. But I want to push the question further, without implying that we should be searching for a single formula. Historians can be expected to disagree among themselves on exactly how the narrative of the nation should be constructed, and even on what the story should primarily be about. Yet widespread appreciation for, if not agreement upon, certain senses of the matter may not be so elusive.

It cannot be repeated often enough that the United States is both a *site* for history and a *player* in history. We can take it for granted that historians need to attend to aspects of history that simply happen "on site" in the United States, as well as aspects of history that are constituted by the United States. But just what do we take the latter to be? Being clear about this may better enable national narrative to flourish without getting in the way of other kinds of history dealing with things that take place in the American site, and vice versa. What is the history of the United States — as opposed to a history of things that happen within it — a history *of?* Answers to this question are implicit in narratives centered on the slavery question, on the frontier, and on the elaboration in America of English institutions. Each of these classic narratives of the United States was a product of its own times. We should not suppose that any narrative we develop will be anything other than a product of ours.

A defensible focus for a national narrative in our own time, I believe, is the notion of *a national solidarity committed — but often failing — to incorporate individuals from a great variety of communities of descent, on equal but not homogeneous terms, into a society with democratic aspirations inherited largely from England.*[22] There is much more to the United States than this. But if one tries to sum up in a single sentence what a national narrative might narrate, this sentence has a number of promising features.

The United States is, indeed, a national solidarity of the kind described. To place emphasis on this fact can serve to reinforce the liberal and cosmopolitan elements of the national self-image without denying the parts of American history that are not liberal and not cosmopolitan. A narrative of this solidarity would have plenty of opportunities to detail the dispersion and consequences of power. It could address episodes in which the nation was a liberating force, a formation that could be called upon to overturn injustices perpetuated by local, regional, and state segments of the nation. But so, too, could such a narrative attend to the episodes of the opposite kind. A national narrative of the sort I envisage here is consistent with, and could easily incorporate, many of the contributions to transnational history published in the *Journal of American History*'s two special issues of September and December 1999, edited by Thelen.[23]

This modest "charter" for national narrative expresses the vital idea that people can be politically equal without being culturally identical, yet it does not suggest that history has enacted this ideal. It acknowledges the individualistic focus of the American polity; individuals, not groups, are incorporated into the nation. Yet the opportunity is there to tell the story of how the boundaries of national solidarity came into being, how and when they were challenged and sometimes changed, and by whom. How has the United States drawn and redrawn its social borders to accommodate, repel, or subjugate this or that group, in defiance of its egalitarian and individualistic self-image? How have groups been defined, and by whom? How has racism and the struggle against it proceeded in a sequences of distinctive settings? This conception of the national story enables the historian to display two truths now vouchsafed to historians, but often resisted by much of the public:

the great extent to which the flourishing of the United States has depended on the exploitation of nonwhites, and the relative weakness, during most of the national history, of egalitarian ideals.

This one-sentence "charter" for a narrative of the United States also acknowledges that the democratic aspirations of the Republic derived primarily—although not exclusively—from England, the specific European country from which virtually all the political leaders of the revolutionary generation directly descended. The declaration of independence impeached the king of England for failing to deliver on what he owed American colonists in their capacity as English nationals, as the king's subjects. To recognize the heavily English foundation of the Constitution of the United States is not to preclude the study of other influences, nor to imply that people today of English descent have any greater personal connection to the constitutional order of the United States than does anyone else. But the reference to England does prevent us from kidding ourselves. Foner is surely correct to begin his *Story of American Freedom* with a section on the complexities of the concept of "The Freeborn Englishman."[24]

Does this vision of the history of the United States lose credibility or appeal if the intended audience is not the American public, but the world? I suspect not. This vision gains much of its appeal from our world-historical situation. Solidarities are being reorganized and retheorized across the planet, and in different directions. I have in mind the proliferation of ethnoreligious nationalisms, the greater standing of human rights organizations purporting to speak for the species and of environmental organizations purporting to speak for the earth, the increasing ordinance of global economic conglomerates, the larger measure of authority exercised by the World Trade Organization, the rise of European identity and the relative diminution of national identity in western Europe, the deterritorialization of identity through the growth of multiple diasporas, the destabilization of ostensibly primordial identity groups by academic theorists, and the breaking down by other academic theorists of the formerly monolithic formation called nationalism into distinctive varieties. The history of the United States achieves some of its world-historical significance in relation to these contemporary transformations, which properly affect our inquiries into the American past. The set of emphases I suggest above may enable more scholars to tell more truths to more people about more of the nation's history as now understood by a global community of professional historians than can other, comparable, one-sentence charters for the national narrative.

Although no single sentence can carry us very far, there are good reasons for forcing ourselves to try a brief formulation. Brevity dramatizes the process by which we define central subjects, how we select certain aspects of an entity's history and deselect others. It encourages us to maintain critical awareness and control over the themes of our narratives. Historians select and deselect with every sentence we write, whether we direct our words to an audience of compatriots, an international learned community, or both, or to any other audience. When we make such choices, as when we make all of the choices entailed by our work, we risk becoming the tools of something, including nations, especially any nation in the destiny of which the historian may wish to play a part, however small. But not all "uses" of historians by nations are equally problematic. Whatever use a historian consciously tries to be to his or her nation, or to any national solidarity, that use is surely best balanced against the imperatives of an international community of scholars for whom the truth is presumably the only client. Hence our two winds of doctrine, if we set our sails right, might yet carry us in the same direction.

4

Money and Academic Freedom
a Half-Century after McCarthyism

Universities amid the Force Fields of Capital

*D*avid, you've managed to insult both the economics department and the
English department at the same time," a colleague told me when I
first delivered this essay as a lecture on my own campus. I've never been sure if
this remark was intended as a compliment or a criticism. But the comment
points to the range of concerns about faculty solidarity and cosmopolitan ideology that I voice here.

The willingness of academics to work together in explaining themselves to
the public that supports them has been vital to the development in the United
States of the largest, most productive, and most independent collection of universities in history. One need not take an uncritical view of these institutions —
any professor can give you a long list of what's wrong with universities in general and with his or her own campus in particular — in order to be concerned
about the preservation of their independence. Yet academics in recent decades
have found it increasingly difficult to agree on what universities are, and how
their purposes should be represented. The solidarity of the professorate is proving difficult to maintain, and the cosmopolitan ideology with which academics

have long defended themselves is no longer as appealing within academia as it once was.

I try to clarify these difficulties in relation to changes in the political economy of research and higher education. I single out the salary policies of universities as a revealing window on this political economy, and observe that universities increasingly pay the most money to those faculty whose careers are the least fully defined by the traditional research and teaching missions of universities, and the least money to those faculty whose careers are the most fully defined by those missions. As faculties and administrators lose confidence in universities as distinctive institutions, they are more inclined to treat universities as collections of instruments for the serving of this or that specific need asserted by one or another extra-academic constituency. I speculate that this spiral of fragmentation may lead to the replacing of universities as we know them with a new set of institutions. There are careers to be advanced and monies to be made in the dismantling of an institution that is, after all, the product of a late-nineteenth-century historical moment long since past.

Even if universities as we know them do survive, the spiral of fragmentation to which I refer makes it more difficult for faculties to work together to defend academic freedom. This difficulty is increased when the threats to academic freedom take forms, as I argue here, very different from those prominent during the McCarthy Era. In our own time the chief threats to academic freedom no longer present themselves as loyalty oaths and political inquisitions. Rather, today's threats are more subtle, and are exercised through monetary incentives and disincentives and through more indirect forms of political pressure. To illustrate the latter, I analyze memorandum written by Lewis Powell in 1971 advocating the use of money and power to make universities more conservative.

Several readers have cautioned that I am too pessimistic about the future of universities, and that I underestimate the capacity of academics to recognize their common interests and to speak forthrightly about what universities do for society. I hope this complaint is proven sound by events. Many faculties, it has been pointed out to me, have rallied to defend their liberties against the constraints embedded in the Patriot Act enacted in the wake of the events of September 11, 2001. This essay was published more than a year before those events, and long before the Patriot Act. But skepticism in the society at large about academia's ability to run its own house seems to be increasing, rather than decreasing. The press is filled with complaints that universities are imbalanced because there are too many liberals and not enough conservatives, and the suggestion is often made that governments and donors need to fix this problem. It is far from clear to me that faculties and administrators will indeed pull together sufficiently to prevent the transferal of more and more de facto authority over academic life to political constituencies and economic interests with little commitment to free inquiry.

What is in special danger of being lost is a respect for academic professionalism and its classical peer review ideology. According to that ideology, any particular disciplinary community exists within what we might see as a series of concentric circles of accountability in an informal but vitally important structure of cognitive authority. This structure of cognitive authority is imperfectly understood by many of academia's critics, yet it is the foundation for "peer-review." In order to maintain its standing in the learned world as a whole, a given community must keep the communities nearest to it persuaded that it is behaving responsibly, and it must also, partly through the support of these neighboring communities, diminish whatever skepticism about its operations might arise in more distant parts of the learned world, and beyond, in the society that scientists and scholars do, after all, serve. So the structure of cognitive authority moves out from particle physics to physics to natural science to science to the learned world as a whole, and then to the most informed members of the public. The farther you get from the technical particulars of the field, the less authority you have to decide what should be going on, but in a democratic society there is some authority distributed all the way out. It is the job of deans and provosts to keep abreast of these trans-disciplinary conversations, and to pressure particular departments and schools to change their way of doing things if the parts of the learned world most qualified to judge are truly dubious about their research programs and their attendant teaching and public service activities.

In this perspective, there is nothing illegitimate about asking for professional accountability as long as it is, indeed, professional. Demanding this accountability need not be the serving as a cat's paw for some external and nefarious authority, "doing their dirty work for them." The learned world owes it to itself, as well as to the society that it serves, to make sure things are done professionally.

Academia as a whole — as one large solidarity — must not neglect this respon-
sibility, as it is sometimes tempted to do, for fear of being seen as someone
else's agents.

Perhaps faculties have a greater capability for solidarity, and for vindicat-
ing cosmopolitanism, than I acknowledge here? I hope so.

This essay was first published in Peggie J. Hollingsworth, ed., Unfet-
tered Expression: Freedom in American Intellectual Life *(Ann*
Arbor: University of Michigan Press, 2000), 161–84.

In 1971 Lewis Powell, then a prominent lawyer in Richmond, Virginia, not yet nominated by President Nixon for the Supreme
Court, outlined a plan for neutralizing liberal and radical professors without running afoul of the academic freedom of individual
faculty. The plan involved the use of money and corporate connections. Powell's memorandum of 1971, to the details of which I
will turn in a moment, is of interest today as an emblem for how
the location of the issue of the political autonomy of universities
has changed during the half-century since the McCarthy era.
Back then, the issue was highly visible in the domain of public
doctrine, where political ideas are policed by state power. Faculty
were purged for holding the wrong views, for being unwilling to
declare their opinions, and for refusing to sign loyalty oaths. Now,
the question of the political autonomy of universities is the most
visible elsewhere: in the force fields of capital, where profit functions like gravity, where knowledge takes the form of property,
where human energy is converted into money, and where values
dance to the sound of markets. It is in that dynamic and multi-
layered space that we may lose what political autonomy universities have managed to achieve and maintain.

Before I turn to the instructive details of the Powell memorandum, I want briefly to remind us of a combination of circumstances that render the political autonomy of universities worth
worrying about and why it is thus necessary for us to locate the
question as precisely as we can. Universities have become more

and more central to the social, cultural, and economic life of the United States, yielding increased pressures to reduce universities to inventories of instruments for this or that interest. Faculties, in the meantime, have become less able to agree on what ethos identifies the university, yielding a diminished capacity to justify to the public the rights and privileges of faculties. Each of these two circumstances—an institution expected to do more and more for society, and a faculty less and less confident about any common purpose—has its own sources. But the two are caught up with each other dialectically. The more tasks that the society persuades or forces universities to accept, the more of a challenge it is for faculties to constitute themselves as a distinctive solidarity. The less able professors are to act together, the more they tend to identify themselves with the constituencies beyond campus—professional, ethnoracial, economic, and political—eager to exploit the university as a tool. This dialectic facilitates the parceling out of the university into a series of relationships between specific segments of the university on the one hand and congruent, specific segments of society on the other.

This dialectic is not new. But it is now intensifying. And it may be unstoppable. It is not clear how many people care about stopping it. Universities with the structure and functions we take for granted are the products of a particular historical moment long since gone. They came into being during the forty years after the Civil War and were adapted gradually over the course of the century just ended. These institutions may be replaced in our new century by a series of new institutions carrying out this or that function currently assigned to universities. Among the apparent harbingers of this future are the transfer of more and more undergraduate instruction into the hands of temporary and part-time faculty, the rise of "virtual universities," the increasing quality and quantity of research carried out in industrial laboratories, the legal and technical capacity of private corporations to create knowledge that belongs only to them, the willingness of some university leaders to undercut the peer review process by lobbying directly with Congress for research grants, and the pressures for profiteering placed on campus administrators by the terms of the Bayh-Dole Act. The whole problem of the political autonomy of universities may disappear, because there will be nothing to be autonomous about.

Perhaps a suspicion to this effect explains a certain timidity in today's efforts to defend universities? Perhaps a sense of inevitability is behind the fact that today's critical discussion of higher education includes no book remotely comparable to Clark Kerr's *The Uses of the University*, which thirty-seven years ago, amid the era of the American university's most prodigious growth, tried to explain in a spirit of confidence and hope what a knowledge-centered institution could do for a democratic society. Whatever one may think of this book, it was not timid. And it really did defend, in terms that made sense at the time, quality higher education for a large public.

Yet universities have virtues that are not yet apparent in the institutions poised to take their place. The effective defense of universities requires political will and a certain amount of solidarity across disciplines and schools. That will and that solidarity seem to me to be in shorter supply now than fifty years ago. Faculty senates were not united in opposition to McCarthyism, but they displayed a degree of unity and an extent of common purpose that is hard to find today. But the challenges of the McCarthy era were radically different from those of our own time. Just how different we can begin to see when we examine the Powell memorandum and its aftermath.

The Powell memorandum originated when a Richmond neighbor and friend of Powell's, an officer of the National Chamber of Commerce, asked Powell's advice on what might be an appropriate agenda for the educational committee of the Chamber.[1] Powell's response was entitled "Attack on American Free Enterprise System," and it summarized this "attack" as including the activities of Ralph Nader and of the people who were bombing banks, all of whom Powell linked to the teachings of such university professors as the University of California at San Diego philosopher Herbert Marcuse. In dealing with this "attack," Powell suggested that *big business*—a term he used in a matter-of-fact way, without irony—finance and direct a comprehensive program of cultural reform designed especially to diminish the influence of liberal and radical university professors. The "imbalance" toward the left found within college and university faculties was, Powell asserted, "the most fundamental problem" facing defenders of the free enterprise system. That Powell believed this—that he believed in the enormous cultural authority of universities and that it was on the political orientation of these institutions that the future of the nation might turn—is itself an interesting feature of his memorandum.

I sometimes wish one of Powell's more sophisticated billionaire friends would have explained to him a basic deal that the journalist Joe Queenan has described. Queenan points out that the way the world works is this:

> Leftist intellectuals with hare-brained Marxist ideas get to control Stanford, MIT, Yale, and the American Studies department at the University of Vermont. In return, the right gets IBM, Honeywell, Disney World, and the New York Stock Exchange. Leftist academics get to try out their stupid ideas on impressionable youths between seventeen and twenty-one who don't have any money or power. The right gets to try out its ideas on North America, South America, Europe, Asia, Australia, and parts of Africa, most of which take Mastercard. The left gets Harvard, Oberlin, Twyla Tharp's dance company, and Madison, Wisconsin. The right gets NASDAQ, Boeing, General Motors, Apple, McDonnell Douglas, Washington D.C., Citicorp, Texas, Coca-Cola, General Electric, Japan, and outer space.

This, adds Queenen, "seems like a fair arrangement."[2] But Powell, being unaware that this deal had been struck, proceeded to outline for the chamber a number of specific measures. All of

these measures involved the calculated use of the money and connections of leading corporations. Among Powell's proposals were
the following, although Powell does not present them in quite the
same order: First, big business should find ways to provide sustained financial support outside the academy for social science
and humanities scholars with sound views. This was a crucial initiative, because these scholars would then enjoy a base independent from the committees that controlled hiring and promotion
in the universities and from the academically dominated review
panels that greatly influenced the dispensing of grant money in
the then-existing public and private agencies. Second, big business
should establish a network of popular speakers and media person-
alities who could effectively popularize the ideas developed by the
scholars. These publicists would write for newspapers and magazines, and, above all, would appear on television, keeping before
the public the National Chamber's perspective on issues of public
policy. Third, big business should lobby trustees and administrators at colleges and universities concerning the political "imbalance" of their faculties, hoping gradually to see more and more
conservative intellectuals integrated into these faculties. Fourth,
big business should urge campus schools of business administration to broaden their curriculum and their role in campus life.
Business schools might even offer their own range of courses to
compete with those offered by departments of political science,
sociology, and history. This initiative would counteract the exclusive claims to academic expertise made by the liberal-dominated
social science departments.

Powell's program included several additional features, beyond
these four. It called for the careful supervision of the writing of
textbooks and of the processes of their adoption by school boards
and administrators. It called for the strict monitoring by the National Chamber of the political content of television programs and
urged that a steady drum beat of complaints be sent to the television networks and to the Federal Communications Commission

objecting to the liberal bias of most television programs. It called for an ideological repositioning of popular magazines, including specifically *Atlantic Monthly, Life,* and *Reader's Digest,* so that editors would publish more articles supportive of the "American way of life." Powell said something should be done about the selection of books on display in corner newsstands and in airports and in drugstores. Too many of the books easily found there were written by such authors as the Black Panther Eldridge Cleaver and the radical Yale law professor Charles Reich, whose *The Greening of America,* long since forgotten, was extravagantly admired and worried about in 1971. In place of such nefarious books, Powell wanted to see prominently on display books written by defenders of the system. But the core of Powell's program related to universities.

Powell's program differed instructively from the best known of earlier efforts to bring under control the apparently subversive influence of professors. Powell was not advocating a ferreting-out campaign, by which any individuals would be targeted for investigation or firing, no matter how repugnant the National Chamber might find their views. Powell did refer to Communists, and he still accepted at face value, and with sincere alarm, the Federal Bureau of Investigation's (FBI's) annual list of what it termed Communist speakers on American campuses. But Powell sketched an approach altogether different from that of red hunters back in the 1940s and 1950s. At no time, even when ranting against the hated and notorious Marcuse, did Powell perpetuate the McCarthyite tradition of calling for the termination of faculty whose ideas Powell found subversive. Even when linking the teachings of campus social scientists and philosophers to the bombings of banks—thirty-nine violent attacks on branches of the Bank of America had been made in the last year and half, Powell reminded the Chamber—Powell never suggested that any action be taken against Marcuse and his kind personally.

Powell's goals, strategy, and tactics were all more sophisticated than those of the McCarthyites. Powell proposed to work through private rather than public channels. And it was no quick fix; it would take many years, Powell said, and it required discipline and patience. It was not a project for "the fainthearted," he warned explicitly. Powell advocated quiet, long-term, carefully planned— dare I use the word *conspiracy?*—to bring about the neutralization of the academic forces he opposed. And, although Powell's program depended on money and position, it was still a strategy more of persuasion than of brute force. To use language Powell did not employ but that I believe captures the relevant distinction, Powell proposed to operate more in the realm of discursive power than in that of juridical power. The goal was to shift the intellectual center of gravity in the social sciences and the humanities, where the curriculum and the content of knowledge had potential relevance to politics. That is where the money and the connections were to be deployed. A crucial aspect of the Powell memorandum, then, is that it assumes that what really matters about professors is their professional intellectual work, not their personal political activities. At no time does Powell even mention the physical or biological sciences or engineering. Back in the McCarthy era, at issue were generally the activities and rights of individual professors, whether their fields had obvious political relevance or not. The Board of Regents of the University of California imposed the loyalty oath on everyone. Powell was not worried about the mechanical engineering professor who had been slow to leave the Communist Party, or the physicist who was friendly with Soviet colleagues, or the chemist who refused on principle to declare his loyalty to the United States.

Powell had a take on academic freedom very different from that of the un-American activities committees of old. Those committees often sneered at the very idea of academic freedom and implied or even asserted that the chief function of academic freedom was to protect scoundrels from justice. In a famous session of the House Un-American Activities Committee (HUAC) in 1953, the counsel for HUAC badgered the University of Chicago historian Daniel J. Boorstin, later destined to become librarian of

Congress, into a humiliating reassurance that the academic free-dom of Boorstin and other witnesses had been infringed in no way by HUAC's investigations of communism on campuses. Powell, by contrast, warned that for big business to attack the principle of ac-ademic freedom would be "fatal" to the program of action Powell was advocating. "Few things are more sanctified in American life than academic freedom," he warned. The chamber could act to advance greater "openness," "fairness," and "balance," ideals that were, he observed, fully consistent with academic freedom.

Indeed, Powell was so concerned about the matter of aca-demic freedom that, even within the presumed privacy of this communication to members of his own tribe, he returned to it re-peatedly. When talking about the textbook aspect of his program he said that what he had in mind was "not an intrusion upon" ac-ademic freedom but "an aide to it." He took a frankly interest-group approach to academic freedom, asserting that "civil rights" organizations had "insisted" on "rewriting many . . . textbooks" and that labor unions, too, had lobbied for textbooks fair to orga-nized labor. It was time for big business to do the same, Powell said. Again, when asking that university trustees and presidents be lobbied to change the political orientation of faculties, Powell told his confidants that this was a delicate project that would backfire if done crudely; he asked that big business work discreetly through alumni groups and trustees to "strengthen" academic freedom by ensuring balance on faculties.

It is important to note that Powell was not asking universities to be disinterested or objective. Powell saw professors as advocates. The problem was that they were advocating the wrong things. Powell's talk about "balance" aimed to put strong conservative voices up against liberal and radical advocates. Powell's objection to Marcuse was not that Marcuse was unprofessional but that Marcuse was advocating the wrong cause.

A few minutes ago I applied to Powell's analysis of the political function of scholarship the Foucaultian distinction between dis-cursive and juridical power, thereby inviting us to see how we might assimilate Powell's thinking into our own conversation about power/knowledge. I want now to call attention to a silence within Powell's memorandum that invites a similar translation. The silence to which I refer is the absence, anywhere in his document, of any sense that universities might have a function other than to support or to undermine a given regime. Powell takes for granted that the university is a set of instruments for interests outside the university. Powell does not employ the terms *oppositional* or *hegemonic* and *counter-hegemonic,* but his memo treats the university purely and simply as an instrument of what many people would colloquially call hegemonic or counter-hegemonic forces. Powell seems to have achieved this view of the world without the help of Marx or Gramsci or Foucault. Powell's silence is far from peculiar to him. I do not want to make Powell sound more like "one of us" than he truly was, but I believe it is fair to say that within the academy during the past few decades there has been a widespread reluctance to assign to universities a positive cultural function unique to them rather than merely in the service of one set or another of economic, ethnoracial, technological, or political interests. This reluctance is often covered by a certain toughness of posture, an unwillingness to appear too idealistic about higher education, a worldly acceptance of the status of the university as a bundle of outcomes rather than as an agent in its own right.

Such studied realism is easy to understand and has much to recommend it. The truths that support this realism are accessible even to the simplest of minds. But the people who built modern universities in the late nineteenth and early twentieth centuries saw beyond these obvious truths. Had those academic pioneers succumbed to this easy realism, had they been incapable of a robust, risk-taking idealism, had they been unwilling to proclaim the university to be an independent cultural agent, they would not have been able to put in place the chief ideological defenses of universities on which we still rely. Universities would not then have achieved the measure of autonomy that they did manage to achieve. One need not romanticize the past or ignore the political and economic matrix of the early growth of American higher education to recognize that a signal accomplishment of the generation of Daniel Coit Gilman, Charles W. Eliot, Andrew Dickson White, and William Rainey Harper is the enormous amount of unrestricted money they obtained for building universities.

Private donors and state legislators were to be persuaded that universities knew what they were doing and could be trusted with money. The builders of American universities, whether public or private, made a great production of the distinctive character of their institutions and of the necessity of letting them chart much of their own future in relation to notions of the society's interests that these academic leaders worked hard to formulate in their own terms. We now find naive and fatuous many of their formulations, and we hasten to distance ourselves from their cloying, Victorian conceits. But their project of maximum autonomy was perpetuated and critically revised by the somewhat less embarrassing Arthur O. Lovejoy and John Dewey and the other professors who founded the American Association of University Professors (AAUP) in 1915, rendering universities yet more autonomous by limiting the discretion through the exercise of which administrators could capitulate to outside political pressures. Without all this, universities would not have come into possession of a tradition of academic freedom strong enough to affect the strategies of people such as Lewis Powell.

Powell outlined a program to which academic freedom's defense of individual faculty rights spoke hardly at all. Money did pour in to conservative think tanks. Television punditry has changed; we have moved from the solitary and ostensibly consensual Eric Sevareid to a pluralistic screen on which we can always expect to see either William Bennett or William Kristol. Some business schools have pursued joint appointments, yielding more and more professors of political science and economics and law and sociology who are also fractionally appointed in schools of business and thus protected by the system of remuneration and peer review maintained by schools of business. Complaints that social scientific and humanities faculties were skewed to the left, that these faculties were not genuinely open to conservative ideas and were unfair in their assessment of conservative job candidates? Such complaints became routine, culminating in the furor over "political correctness." Centers and institutes designed to circumvent if not to discredit the university-based disciplinary establishments? The Olin Foundation, the Manhattan Institute, the Heritage Foundation, the Witherspoon Foundation, and the Free Press are among the organizations often associated with such efforts. None of this just happened. A merit of the Powell memorandum is that it constitutes evidence of how clear and calculating was some of the thought behind this campaign.

But it would be absurd to attribute this campaign to Powell personally. He was not the only one thinking along these lines. The columnist Jack Anderson soon made Powell's memorandum public, in any case, after Nixon nominated Powell for the Supreme Court. The National Chamber itself then published the document in its own house organ. It would be equally absurd, and I now enter a second disclaimer made necessary by my breezy use of the Powell memorandum, to imply that everything in universities that Powell disliked should be defended just because Powell disliked it. Some would even insist that the real threat to academia's autonomy has not been big business but faculty colleagues whose persistent foolishness rendered universities more vulnerable in a political environment to which these colleagues were irresponsibly oblivious. Another disclaimer: the social science and humanities departments of our universities have not exactly folded under the pressure of the program outlined by Powell. Although the charges of political correctness have done some real damage to the standing of universities with the public, I do not see much evidence that hiring committees have compromised their judgments about what counts as excellent scholarship to bring more conservatives into departments of English, philosophy, and sociology. Whatever the lobbyists of big business may have accomplished through their pressure on universities, one goal that seems to have eluded them is diminishing the power of disciplinary peer review in the hiring process.

Yet the Powell memorandum is at least an artifact of the migration of the question of the political autonomy of universities. Once visible chiefly in the juridical space where the political ideas and conduct of individuals are policed by the state but are protected by classical academic freedom doctrine, the question is now the most importantly located where Powell was more comfortable with it: in the company of money, in relatively unregulated economic space, where classical academic freedom doctrine is less relevant. There, economic incentives and disincentives for certain kinds of work are presented to individual faculty, to research groups, to departments, to entire schools, and to whole campuses. And anyone who has had the slightest contact with the fundraising aspects of universities today knows that plenty of people with money are thinking about just what can be done with these incentives and disincentives.

Academic priorities have always been set in economic contexts and no doubt always will be. When I invoke the generation of Daniel Coit Gilman and Andrew Dickson White and William Rainey Harper and refer to the relative lack of restrictions on the funds they obtained from Johns Hopkins and Ezra Cornell and John D. Rockefeller and other industrialists, I certainly do not mean that all that went on in an economic vacuum. It is a matter of degree. At issue is the authority exercised by universities as corporate entities in responding to economic contingencies and the principles that govern the exercise of that authority. Can universities maintain a value system in some tension with the value system of the commercial marketplace? How much tension? I do not know exactly how this tension should be managed, and I will not pretend to have worked out much of a program to deal with the challenges to which I am here calling attention. But I am convinced of at least two things: I am convinced that the bulk of today's academic leadership is not thinking systematically about this issue and is going with the flow. And I am convinced that one place to observe this tension between academia's value system and that of the commercial marketplace of the surrounding society is the salary policy of universities.

I focus on salary policy because this happens to be an arena in which we can view, relatively unobstructed, the operation of academic corporate authority in relation to the commercial marketplace. And in salary policy we find compelling evidence that the gap is closing between what universities value and what is valued in the commercial marketplace.

Faculty salaries in the United States have never been as uniform as they remain even today in many of the European universities, where the government often sets a flat rate for everyone. Modest salary differentials are part of the tradition in the United States. But the tradition also includes what we might call "medical school exceptionalism." Medical school salaries have been much higher on the grounds of "opportunity costs." Higher salaries were needed to attract men and women who could be out there healing the sick and billing for their services. Certain other highly paid professions created similar conditions. Exceptionalism spread to law schools. Yet the University of California long resisted law school exceptionalism in the name of cross-campus equity and did not formally adopt a special scale for law until 1969. Engineering and business followed suit. The University of California's special scale for Schools of Engineering and Business was phased in during the early 1980s, giving de jure status to salary differentials by school that had long since been de facto.

In our present historical moment, as confidence in the university as a distinctive workplace declines and as the university increasingly appears to be merely a site for careers defined in other arenas, the argument for salary equity across departments and school loses the force it once had. If some biologists in science departments are doing work similar to that done in medical schools, some ask, why not extend medical school exceptionalism to biology? A vivid index of the decline of faculty solidarity is the willingness of universities nationally to tolerate increasing salary differentials by field for faculty of equal merit as judged by peer review within each field. I am not talking about the pros and cons of the star system. I am talking about institutional decisions to take entire fields and pay a lot more money to people in those fields than to colleagues of comparable stature in other fields.

I am going to cite some figures from a survey of salaries in effect during the 1998–99 academic year at Harvard, Yale, Princeton, Columbia, Massachusetts Institute of Technology, Stanford, and California Institute of Technology. I selected these seven because I found that they were the ones with whom my own campus, Berkeley, was most often forced to compete for our best faculty. The average salary for full professors of economics at those universities — taken together — was revealed to be $122,000. This figure does not count summer ninths and research accounts. Nor, of course, does this figure include consulting fees and other forms of private remuneration that depend to some extent on the standing one enjoys as a result of holding a professorship at a prestigious university. The average full professor's salary in the same institutions for faculty of the same age and career stage was $104,000 in the basic science disciplines and $98,000 in the humanities.

Part of the significance of these last two figures is that humanities professors, generally paid the lowest salaries, have remained fairly close to their comparably distinguished colleagues in mathematics and physics and chemistry at the most prestigious of the research universities. The gap is considerably greater at universities of lesser prestige. The general rule is that the less stature the institution has by prevailing indicators, the greater the gap between the sciences and the humanities in basic salary. Also, the summer ninths common in the sciences and rare in the humanities render the comparison somewhat misleading. But the gap between scientists and humanists on the one hand and economics on the other is enormous. A greater gap separates business administration from everyone else in the same survey: business professors logged in at $144,000. At the level of an entering assistant professor, moreover, it is not uncommon for a recruit in business administration to be offered a salary of $100,000, while a comparably qualified recruit in mathematics or history will be offered a salary of $45,000 or even less. New assistant professors of economics, too, are often hired at salaries twice that of comparably qualified entry-level colleagues in English, psychology, philosophy, or anthropology. The same pattern applies to the salaries of deans. Those heading commercially relevant professional schools, such as law and business, are paid much more than deans of arts and sciences.

A consistent pattern is that faculty whose academic skills are of the sort that enable them to make the most money on the side, without resigning their professorships, are also the people to whom universities are willing to pay the highest salaries. This tendency is becoming more pronounced each year. It is seen in the remarkable escalation of salaries in the fields of economics, business administration, law, biotechnology, and computer science. At the same time, those faculty whose careers are the most fully centered in universities, and who have the least opportunity to generate private income through consulting and other outside activities, are the ones to whom universities pay the least. A young economist only a few years beyond the Ph.D. who has published but a handful of papers may be awarded a higher annual salary than a distinguished midcareer mathematician who has won the Field Medal or than a senior humanist who has served as poet laureate of the United States. A garden-variety professor in several of the professional schools can expect to receive two summer ninths every year as a matter of course, whereas some of the most accomplished professors of German literature or of art history may go twenty years with only an occasional summer ninth, and then usually for performing a time-consuming service. The same pattern extends even to staff support. Campuses frequently tolerate extraordinary variations, yielding much higher levels of staff support in certain professional schools able to raise the money and in grant-oriented science units. Overhead is not distributed equally but tends to go to those who, as they say, "earn" it. The pattern is rendered all the more problematic when student enrollment figures are taken into account. The faculty groups paid the most have the smallest number of students. Schools of business and law are dramatic examples of the combination of low faculty-student ratios and exceptionally high salaries.

What happens, then, is this: *universities pay the most money to faculty whose careers are the least defined by the research and teaching mission of universities and pay the least money to those faculty whose careers are the most fully defined by the universities' research and teaching missions.* This is the reality that I wish more of our academic leaders would confront and address. What presidents and provosts generally prefer to do is to fall into old routines about the differences between the sciences and the humanities, which is not at issue. By diverting us into that old science-versus-humanities conversation what solidarity faculties may retain gets diminished all the more. Presidents and provosts need to be forthright about the centrality of basic science, humanities, and social science to universities and to guard against the further fragmentation of this arts-and-science core.

To be sure, no single campus, no matter how fearless its president and its deans, can fight this battle alone. The pattern is national. Any individual university that tries to go against the trend will lose out to universities willing to revise their salary policies in the direction of the non-academic marketplace. But national academic leaders find this matter beyond their control, too. I have talked with a number of university presidents about this problem, and I see little evidence that anything is being done about it.

"Opportunity costs" are instantly cited, and to "ignore" them is to be "naive." Yet it is interesting to contemplate what might

happen if our leaders formed a cabal. Perhaps Lee Bollinger and
Harold Shapiro and Robert Berdahl and Neil Rudenstine and a
number of other presidents could come to a friendly agreement.
Sherman Anti-Trust Act be damned! If the airlines can do it, why
not our Lee and Harold? Our captains of the academic industry
might promise each other that none of their institutions would
pay economists more than a certain dollar amount. If Texas Tech
University will not join in the agreement, some of our leading
economists can ponder the prospects of a move to Lubbock.

I hope our colleagues in economics and at Texas Tech can for-
give this bit of levity, but it remains to be seen whether universities
will prove able to define themselves as a sufficiently corporate entity to defend more than a shred of the old tradition of salary equity. According to that tradition, being on a faculty, rather than
being part of a transacademic profession, is the primary context
in which merit judgments are translated into dollars. Faculties
themselves are honestly divided about salary policy. Some regard
as anachronistic the very idea that academia is so distinctive a
realm. These colleagues doubt that a university is marked off sufficiently from Dow Chemical or Bell Laboratories or Price Water-
house or Cravath Swain or the *Washington Post* to justify the reluctance of campuses to move yet further toward matching industrial
salary offers. I have heard more than one professional school dean
at Berkeley observe that academic salaries are not high enough to
bring on to our faculty those experienced practitioners whose
ability to instruct students in the workaday profession makes their
hiring a priority for their school. The students want to learn not
from someone who "has only studied it," these deans report, but
from someone who has "really done it." The striking implication
here is that the line between the professional school and the profession should be even less sharp than it now is and that location in
a university is only a minor part of professional training.

If salary policy affords a relatively unobstructed view of the
gradual acceptance by universities of the values of the commercial

marketplace, we at least know, as a result of what we see there, what to look for when we scrutinize research policy. I am not going to say much about research policy because this topic is already generating a reasonable amount of critical discussion. The *Atlantic* recently carried an extensive discussion of it. I recommend "The Kept University," by Eyal Press and Jennifer Washburn,[3] but I find it significant that the lead for discussing these matters publicly is more often taken by journalists than by academic administrators. This supports my sense that the people with the most institutionalized responsibility for identifying and dealing with major crises in academia are not as engaged as they should be.[4]

Yet when dealing with research policy, as opposed to salary policy, it is not always easy to agree on what counts as evidence of our autonomy. This difficulty is seen even in so well studied an aspect of recent academic history as federal funding of academic research during the cold war. Universities accepted billions upon billions of federal dollars given in the name of national defense, but universities were far from passive. Rebecca S. Lowen's *Creating the Cold War University*, a recent book about Stanford, shows that university officials acted consciously and systematically to take advantage of federal dollars.[5] One cannot say that Stanford failed to exercise authority as a corporate entity. Although Lowen argues that defense money turned Stanford in certain directions and away from others, some observers would insist that provosts and deans at Stanford, Harvard, Berkeley, and elsewhere took wise advantage of the National Defense Education Act and other opportunities to build programs in science and in foreign languages that were academically warranted and demand no apology. Had academic leaders not made such skillful use of federal defense dollars, the argument might proceed, universities would not have been powerful enough to worry Powell in 1971.

For all the similarities between private and federal funding of university research, there is one important difference, however, that, at the risk of belaboring the obvious, can be underscored here. The aims behind federally funded research, and the various guidelines that attend upon federal grants, have been decided on through a political process that has at least some connection to democracy and to the public interest. Insofar as universities are operating in the public interest, as I believe they should, and insofar as universities must respect the decisions of democratically elected representatives of the public, as I believe they must, the priorities embedded in federal dollars are *in principle* less at odds with the mission of universities than are the priorities embedded in dollars provided by profit-seeking corporations. This is not to deny that massive federal support of certain kinds of research and not others may have greater overall influence on the direction of universities than private funding, nor is it to deny that federal funding is often guided by the priorities of powerful private interests in the society. It is only to call attention to a principle that renders vigilance about private funding all the more important on the grounds of basic democratic theory. Hence a ratcheting up of vigilance on behalf of free inquiry and the public interest is justified at this historical moment, when private capital is positioned to play a greater role than ever in determining the future of universities. Public universities, especially, are at risk of being significantly transformed by the combination of diminished state support for "elite" academic programs and increased dependence on private donors.

The vigilance to which I refer is potentially divisive. Indeed, any effort to confront directly the question of the political autonomy of universities at this time will take place within the dialectic to which I referred at the outset. The more extensive, dispersed, and particularistic become the interests to which we are asked to respond, the more problematic becomes our inability to state clearly to ourselves and to the public what we are; the less able we are to act in concert and to defend ourselves as a corporate entity, the more we risk falling into random and ad hoc responses to the economic incentives and disincentives that surround us.

The development of a coherent and compelling vindication of universities will not go very far toward meeting the challenge of political autonomy in our time. It is only a start. Yet this modest step is not being taken. I am not persuaded that universities are being defended as well as they might be. Most administrative leadership, by focusing narrowly on the economic contributions universities make to localities, regions, states, and the nation, gives away too much. We thus invite the narrowing of the criteria by which universities are held accountable and we encourage the economic beneficiaries of universities to exercise greater control over their shape and orientation. This problem is especially acute in public universities.

While most university presidents run on about the contributions universities make to the economy, the modest project of clarifying the character and role of the university for the public has been inhibited by the humanities parochialism that dominates public discussion of higher education by professors. Professors are doing very little to right the balance. Indeed, one savant after another taking stock of academia turns out to pay no attention whatsoever to the physical and biological sciences, to say nothing of the professional schools. This makes it all the easier for presidents and provosts to ignore the ranting of humanists as the naive effusion of people who have no understanding of the political economy of science. David Damrosch's *We Scholars*, Zachary Karabell's *What Is College For?*, Bill Readings's *The University in Ruins*, and a steady stream of essays in *Critical Inquiry* and other learned quarterlies all treat universities as if they consisted mainly of English departments.[6] Even when the role of literary studies is indicated as the specific topic of discussion, the argument is usually expressed in terms of a diagnosis of and prescription for the university as a whole. What's good for English is assumed to be good for all. If English professors doubt something, then no one in the world has any business taking it seriously. The ignorance of American humanists about the circumstances under which their colleagues in molecular biology and chemical engineering work is appalling and makes it exceedingly difficult to expect that colleagues in the natural sciences will make common cause with humanists in defense of their shared interests in the autonomy of the universities.

This humanities parochialism is manifest in the current enthusiasm for a university "based on dissensus." Eschewing "the search for consensus" as impossible in the wake of multicultural insights into the world's diversity and postmodern insights into the relativity of knowledge, some of our humanists call for a "community of dis-sensus" devoted to the presentation of "irreconcilable" and "mutually opaque goods." The very ideal of knowledge would be downplayed in favor of the ideal of respect, declares J. Hillis Miller, arguing, ostensibly, on the basis of a global outlook critical of American nationalism and Western imperialism. The mission of the new university would be to respect difference and to use the reality of difference to resist the "totalizing forces" of technology and the global capitalist economy. There appears to be nothing frivolous in Miller's abandonment of the whole idea that better knowledge about the world might enable us to cope with it more effectively. Yet there is something suspect, if not downright phony, about a call for a new consensus around the ideal of dissensus. The shared understanding of the evidence and reasoning by which dissensus should be preferred constitutes a consensus as demanding as any other. And I wonder how much attention we owe to discussants who betray no interest in what the ideal of dissensus would do to science departments, or even social science departments, and who, while urging us to build a university of dissensus, are capable of offering such bland and complacent afterthoughts as the following: "It is difficult to imagine," allows a pensive J. Hillis Miller, "how such a university would or should be organized, how it would be administered, who would decide how funds should be allotted, and how its accomplishments in teaching and research would be measured."[7]

Miller underestimates our capacity for agreeing on what counts as good scholarship and science, even in the social scientific and humanistic fields, where agreement is inevitably more elusive. By underestimating this capacity, Miller and his kind diminish a credibility with the public and with each other that we have a right to claim, and they ignore a basis for internal academic solidarity that we very much need. We often hear it said that disciplines and subdisciplines in the social sciences and the humanities have no effective standards for evaluating scholarship, that "anything goes," that internal intellectual conflicts mock as fraudulent the whole idea of scholarly consensus. These complaints miss the mark.

Three years of scrutinizing the reports of search committees and tenure committees and stacks of letters solicited for merit reviews at Berkeley[8] have led me to the conclusion that the old peer review system still works remarkably well for identifying intellectual excellence, even in disciplines and subdisciplines in which conflicts over basic theoretical questions are genuine and deep. This capacity for agreement about intellectual merit is masked, however, by real disagreements, and more often by uncertainties, about two other things: first, the intellectual direction in which a particular program should go, and, second, the extent to which academic decisions should respond to this or that social interest. Many of the most severely split votes in appointment and tenure cases, and many of the dossiers of outside letters displaying the greatest disparities in merit assessment, turn out on close scrutiny to reflect disagreements about these other questions.

Does a given scholar's direction suit a particular unit's current needs as well as those needs might be served by a scholar of equal merit who worked on something else? To what extent should the university use its hiring and promotion actions to help remedy the social prejudices that have resulted in the historic underrepresentation in the academy of certain groups of people? Given the severity of this or that social pathology, especially within one's state or region, how important is it that we have on our faculty people who study that pathology? Given the value to the campus of a certain private foundation's support, how important is it that this foundation's nonbinding expectations about a given faculty position or program be honored? Such questions, I am saying, are matters of frequent uncertainty and disagreement. Pretending to assess intellectual merit while actually responding to one or more of these other issues generates the impression that disciplines and subdisciplines are less functional than they are.

I do not want to exaggerate the distinction between questions about scholarly merit and questions about program direction and social responsibility. Being committed to the exploration of what the salient research community regards as "the right questions" is of course part of a merit evaluation. And I certainly do not want to present too positive a picture of the capacity of scholars to behave professionally. Accusing ourselves of collective bad faith, as Terry Eagleton recently observed, has become a mark of good character.[9] I would not want to be thought seriously deficient in that regard.

But distinguishing these two sorts of issues—the one about the intellectual merit of a scholar's work and the other about the role that universities should play in society—may even help us to engage more productively our disagreements about issues of the second variety. The most helpful engagement with these issues known to me is a book of 1996 entitled *The Future of Academic Freedom*, edited by Louis Menand. Most contributors to this book take for granted that the political autonomy of universities is the central foundation for academic freedom and that political autonomy depends on the credibility with which universities can represent themselves as something more than a set of instruments in the service of regimes and counter-regimes defined outside academia. Edward Said, Thomas Haskell, Joan Scott, and other contributors predicate the political autonomy of universities on a distinctive ethical practice they attribute to scientists and scholars. This book may not be to our own time what Kerr's *The Uses of the University* was to its time, but so far as I am concerned it is the best thing going. I want to call attention to the essay of Edward Said because it is driven by a cosmopolitan preoccupation with the same diversities in modern life that led Reading, Miller, Francois Lyotard, and others to the ideal of "dissensus." Said, himself a professor of English, offers a bracing repudiation of humanities parochialism.

What defines the academic "calling," as Said describes it with unabashed idealism, is "the unending search for truth," which entails "a particular process of inquiry, discussion, and exchange" not exclusive to colleges and universities but not "encountered as regularly outside as inside the academy."[10] Said believes in plain talk about truth and knowledge. Now, Said does not need to be instructed that "truth" is a contested concept and that inquiry takes place within a matrix of power, but he will not yield the vocabulary of *veritas* to his enemies. Said is one of the anglophone world's most conspicuous and accomplished critics of the epistemic arrogance and cultural imperialism sometimes said to be indissoluably bound up with truth talk. Said, the scourge of "Orientalism" and of a host of Eurocentric conceits, and a formidable critic of models of knowledge that presuppose an eternally existing truth to which we can gain unmediated access, is determined to salvage from the discourse wars *a vocabulary with which the academy can communicate honestly with the public.*

But Said is less worried about the hermeneutic preciousness of his colleagues—always putting the word *truth* in quotation marks—than about the danger that some of them will relinquish valuable ideals, including academic freedom itself, because these ideals have been tainted when used to protect right wingers and racists and because these ideals have been invoked by Alan Bloom and by those who have lambasted the liberal arts academy for political correctness. Said, who can scarcely contain his contempt for Bloom, worries that defenders of diversity who share his disgust

with Bloom will be so shortsighted as to yield the ideal of academic freedom to Bloom and his kind rather than to claim it for
their own and be willing to struggle over its meaning.

And struggle Said is prepared to do, not only against the Alan
Blooms of this world but also against other apostles of what he
sees as narrowness, including, especially, those who make a production in an academic setting of their ethnoracial and national
identities. "We should think of academic freedom," Said insists in
the climactic passage of his essay, not as invitation to develop and
indulge particularistic identities but "as an invitation to give up
on" the identities that claim us outside the academy. Central to
the culture of universities for Said is a commitment to truth as
one's primary client and to a community of inquiry just as deep
and wide as we can make it. Knowledge, insists Said, is not a function of the identities we bring to inquiry but is something for
which we put such identities at *"risk."*[11] For Said, universities are
agents of cosmopolitanism, and the foundation for faculty solidarity is a commitment to cosmopolitan ideals.

Now, Said is far from the first to associate universities with cosmopolitanism. Indeed, one of the arresting features of his formulation of cosmopolitanism is the ease with which it can be mapped
on top of the classical ideology of science as developed by Charles
Peirce during the era of the development of modern universities.
Peirce emphasized the dependence of knowledge on imperfect
communities of human knowers rather than on the properties of
the world itself. Although Pierce was inspired by the physical sciences, the ethic of inquiry he proposed applied throughout the
realm of belief, including what we now call the social sciences and
humanities.[12]

Hence the intellectual viability and strategic appeal of Saidian
cosmopolitanism as an academic ideology are enhanced by the
ease with which it can be assimilated into a set of dispositions sanctioned by tradition within the academic world and across the lines
that separate scientists from humanists. And cosmopolitanism is

an ideal for universities that a substantial portion of the public—even, perhaps, a suspicious public—might actually understand and appreciate.[13] This hope may be vain, but Lewis Powell himself gives us at least slight reason to entertain it.

I invoke Powell near the end of this lecture because there is another incident in his career that involves academic freedom and the question of the political autonomy of universities and that even involves a hint of cosmopolitanism. In the *Bakke* case of 1978, Powell wrote an opinion that is generally credited with providing the constitutional foundation for affirmative action. Universities could take ethnoracial categories into account among other considerations, wrote Powell, in the interests of cultural diversity. It was the cosmopolitanizing, deprovincializing functions of universities on which Powell's reasoning in the *Bakke* case was founded.

I want to call attention not only to the incipient cosmopolitanism of Powell's call for campuses that displayed and explored a great range of "ideas and mores" but also to Powell's simultaneous defense of the political autonomy of universities. It is because of the principle of academic freedom, argued Powell, that universities must be left great latitude to decide their own admissions policies. And if, in the context of that autonomy, universities choose to promote cultural diversity, there is no constitutional prohibition on their doing just that.

It may be ironic that the man who saved affirmative action in universities—for twenty years, at least—was the same Virginia lawyer who seven years before had plotted for the political neutralization and transformation of faculties. But Powell's two engagements with universities and academic freedom, whatever else we may learn from considering them together, can remind us of the complexity of our relationship with those who are skeptical about us and can remind us that searching for common ground is not always a mistake.

5

Enough Already

Universities Do Not Need More Christianity

*H*as the cosmopolitanism espoused by the academic community of the
United States in the process of its liberation from Protestant cultural
*hegemony taken us too far from the needs of a society that is, after all, about 85
percent Christian? I do not think so. In this intervention in the religion-and-
higher-education debates I try to convince religiously affirming colleagues that
all of us in the academic community—be we Christians or atheists or Muslims or whatever—are better off reinforcing the rules of secular inquiry than
bending those rules to pay more homage to Christianity. We better serve society
as a whole by holding to this hard-won independence.*

*The immediate context for this intervention was my participation in a
three-year consultation convened by the Lilly Foundation in the late 1990s.
Hence this piece refers several times to the dynamics of "the Lilly Seminar."
But the issues go well beyond the Lilly group, and in our new century are being
pressed nationally and in many local settings by an increasingly vocal and in-
sistent religious lobby. The blind spots and evasions that troubled me in the
conversations of the Lilly group are sufficiently widespread to invite the inclusion of this piece in* Cosmopolitanism and Solidarity.

*My emphasis here does not imply that the religious aspects of American
history have been adequately handled by my professional colleagues. I have*

often complained in other venues (e.g., in "Jesus Matters in the USA," Modern Intellectual History, April 2004, and "Among the Believers," Harper's, November 2004) that the history of religion in general and of twentieth century Christianity in particular has been wrongly marginalized by too many members of my own profession. One need not affirm something in order to study it, and to recognize its presence in history. I also believe that too many secular intellectuals have been needlessly rude to religious believers and insensitive to the vast differences in belief within the ranks of Christians, especially the differences between evangelicals and liberals. Yet upon trying earnestly and repeatedly to engage faith-affirming academics, my frustrations have mounted, and my own free-thinking predilections have been reinforced.

Two tendencies among my interlocutors are especially frustrating to me. One is a willful refusal to confront honestly the honorable reasons men and women have had over the course of the last two centuries for rejecting Christian commitment, or drifting away from it, or restricting it to a private realm. If Christianity is basically right, and its hold on the North Atlantic West justified by its truth value, the logic of this willful refusal proceeds, then its decline among the intelligentsia must be the result of misunderstanding or fraud. A second source of frustration for me is a reluctance to acknowledge how intimately and persistently the affirmation of Christian values by faculties and administrators has been historically bound up with discrimination against Jews, and in blatant forms as recently as the 1940s. When a prominent professor of Christian ethics accused me of being a "secular triumphalist" I responded by asking if she could offer a non-triumphalist narrative of the integration of Jews into American universities after World War II and she gazed at me with bland incomprehension.

This intervention was first published in Andrea Sterk, ed., Religion, Scholarship, and Higher Education: Perspectives, Models, and Future Prospects *(Notre Dame: University of Notre Dame Press, 2002), 40–49.*

Universities have reason to be proud of having created, within the most Christian of all industrialized societies of the North Atlantic West, a rare space in which ideas identified as Christian are not implicitly privileged. Our leading colleges and universities once shared in a pervasive Protestant culture, to which they owe a great deal. Now, however, mainstream academia maintains a certain critical distance from the Christian project. This critical distance is consistent with the drift of science and scholarship in the North Atlantic West. Not everyone is happy about this critical distance. The very topic "Religion and Higher Education" generally carries an implication that something is amiss. Higher education has gone too far in a secular direction, it is sometimes complained, and now pays too little respect to religious commitment in general and to Christian commitment in particular. I find this complaint hard to credit.

In defending mainstream academia's critical distance from Christian commitment here, I will not be suggesting that the men and women who are caught up in secular academia's workings are able always to live by the rules of fairness they espouse. Nor is my point that modern learning has so fully exhausted the intellectual resources of the classical religious traditions that it can responsibly pay no attention to them. I stress these disclaimers because I find that anyone who resists the movement to bring more Christian commitment back into academia is accused of being an uncritical defender of the status quo. *At issue, rather, is whether these imperfect academic communities can be improved by diminishing the critical distance from Christian cultural hegemony that they have achieved only after a long struggle.*

I put the question in this way because without this question there turns out to be little to discuss. I assert this with some conviction after three years of conversation within the admirably collegial Lilly Seminar. The overwhelming majority of the members of this seminar displayed a commitment to Christianity (I believe I was one of only four out of thirty who did not). Within this majority, a great many displayed a persistent if elusively articulated sense that American higher education was too aloof from religious commitment. Just where and how is this aloofness problematic?

To this question the seminar was not able to come up with a coherent, agreed-upon answer. Of specific complaints from one concerned Christian or another there was no shortage, but most of these complaints proved too weak to generate sustained support even from coreligionists. Everyone in the seminar agreed, to be sure, that crude religion bashing could not be defended, that the serious academic study of religion should be higher than it now is on the agenda of several scholarly disciplines, and that this society needs a variety of kinds of institutions of higher education, including some that are religiously affiliated. And almost everyone agreed, after some friendly interrogation, that Christians were so well treated in the United States, even in elite academia, that it was a mistake to represent Christians as "victims." Many of the seminar's most animated discussions were well off the topic. It was common to grouse about this or that aspect of contemporary American academic life—its failure to live up to its own stated ideals was a favorite theme of some—but eventually someone would point out that what we were discussing was not much related to religion.

So, one might ask, what's all this about? The Lilly group was a seminar in search of a problem. But every now and then the search succeeded. In almost every such moment, a close reading of the transcripts will confirm, the problem proved to be some version of the question I have italicized above. Here, in this postseminar volume, I want to sketch several of the arguments I made during the seminar. In so doing, I will voice a skeptical perspective on the higher-education-and-religion conversation as it is now being pursued in the United States.

Many of those who want to reform academia in a more religious direction turn out, upon scrutiny, to be hoping to change the structure of plausibility taken for granted by the prevailing epistemic communities, but are slow to articulate and defend this program of reform. This initiative should be brought out into the open and debated. To do so, we need to begin with a familiar distinction.

Motivation and warrant; origins and verification; discovery and justification. These are three versions of an old distinction about science and scholarship that was drawn too sharply by the logical positivists, and by some of the theorists who preached against "the genetic fallacy." We now are quick to acknowledge that our decisions about what shall count as a standard for true belief may owe something to what motivates us to make a claim, or to hope that the claim may be proven true. And we are quick to acknowledge, too, that the prevailing modes of warrant in the epistemic community within which we work may also become part of our motivation for advancing a claim: we may be motivated to advance certain ideas because they are likely to be found true within a community whose approval we desire. But once these and other such caveats are entered against the old distinction, it can serve us well when we talk about religion and contemporary learned communities.

The personal circumstances of any individual inquirer exercise an important influence over what topics he or she will pursue and what approaches to those topics he or she will find attractive. There is no reason to doubt or lament this fact about inquiry. An individual's religious orientation may help to motivate an inquiry, a working hypothesis, and/or a specific claim one hopes to vindicate. But when it comes to warranting the claims made, what matters most are the rules, formal and tacit, of the relevant epistemic community. Those rules are of course contingent, and often contested. But that such rules exist, and are important, will be understood by anyone who has sat on a journal's editorial board, served on a prize committee, attended a tenure meeting, dispensed grant money, or helped an academy decide who should be elected to membership. If those rules fail to reflect a given religious orientation, then that religious orientation loses its salience in the warranting process. Even if an individual organization or a particular group finds that biblical evidence, or the evidence of immediate religious experience, helps to convince them of a particular truth, other kinds of evidence will be required to persuade the larger epistemic community of sociologists or physicists or historians.

I stress the cogency of this simple distinction between motivation and warrant because so many people have proven eager to avoid it. Often, the initiative to change warranting rules is obscured when a Christian believer says he or she simply wants to be able to declare a worldview openly. That sounds like an affirmation of a motive, and a request to be heard sympathetically when one affirms the motive publicly. When asked if this is all that's meant—when invited, that is, to accept the distinction between motivation and warrant, and to keep religion on the one side of it—some will see the point and say, "yes, the warranting process, if it is to work in a community that includes nonbelievers as well as believers, must operate by that community's structure of plausibility." Fair enough. Yet others will equivocate. It's "more complicated," they will say. They will complain that the rules of the mainstream academic communities are too narrow. There almost always follows a call for "tolerance," for a more "pluralistic" setting in which a variety of outlooks are entertained.

Pluralism in this context usually means accepting forms of evidence and reasoning that were once plausible within disciplinary communities in the social sciences and humanities but are no longer. There was once a time when scholars in the North Atlantic West took for granted a shared Christianity. In that bygone era, the boundaries of the epistemic community and the boundaries of the community of faith were largely coterminous. But now the boundaries of the epistemic communities that define discussion in the learned world are no longer coterminous with the Christian community of faith, and this fact appears to create discomfort on the part of some Christians. There are good reasons, too obvious in the intellectual history of the last three hundred years to bear repeating here, why the prevailing epistemic communities now have the boundaries that they do, and why these communities, as a consequence of their relative de-Christianization, no longer count biblical evidence and other religious experience particular to Christianity as relevant to the assessment of a truth-claim or an interpretation. At issue, then, is not whether learned communities should be tolerant or intolerant, pluralistic or nonpluralistic, flexible or inflexible, open or repressive; at issue rather is the specific direction the always ongoing revision of the epistemic rules of these communities should take.

An incident that took place during a meeting of the Lilly Seminar can illustrate the importance of the motivation-warrant distinction, and can also illustrate the ease with which this distinction can be obscured or evaded by well-meaning discussants who are eager to get Christianity more involved in the academic process. A speaker criticized the political science discipline, and presented his critique as growing directly out of his Catholic commitment. I asked him to specify the relevance of Catholicism to the critique. Was it simply a personal context in which he had developed the critique, and indeed a motive for thinking in this direction? Was the critique one that only Catholics would be able to develop? Could non-Catholics accept the critique (it was manifest by this time that many non-Catholics in the room accepted the critique, so the significance of this question was all the more apparent)? Could the critique be justified on grounds that had nothing whatsoever to do with Catholicism? If the latter was the relevance of Catholicism not confined to the context of motivation and largely irrelevant to the context of warrant?

The speaker and several others struggled for some time with these questions. Several were determined to keep Catholics in possession of the critique, while eager to see it shared with the rest of the world. Eventually, one position won strong support in the group. It was as follows. Sure, non-Catholics can appreciate and make use of this critique, but if they detach it from the matrix out of which it came they will be failing to credit Catholicism for producing the critique. Catholicism is the inspiration for something valued by the larger community; hence the nurturing of Catholicism is in the interests of the larger community. We do not want to cut off this source of inspiration, which might happen if we neglected the tree from which the fruit was picked. This tree is likely to bear other good fruit. The questions I had raised, while provocative, were beside the point. What really mattered was the connection between good ideas and their matrix.

This position is remarkable in several respects. First, it invites the retort that when ideas we like come from matrices we dislike we do not make the nourish-the-tree argument. An example is the Nazi campaign against cancer and tobacco, many features of which prefigured programs that are now counted as wholesome in medical and public health communities of the United States. We do not say, "Hey, this cancer breakthrough shows that the Nazi tree could bear good fruit, so let's see if trees of the fascist species bear other good fruit in regard to, say, race or retardation or government organization." Second, the position does not take into account the possibility that a lot of non-Catholics might have come up with the same ideas on their own, which would diminish the argument for watering the Catholic tree. The harvest of many orchards needs to be assessed before we can be sure just where our agricultural energies are best spent. Third, the position takes no account of the distressing possibility that when the entirety of the cherished tree or orchard's harvest is assessed, it will be found to produce as much noxious fruit as sweet. Most matrices for cultural production have negative as well as positive potential. Fourth, the position finesses the motivation-warrant issue by (a) agreeing that the critique might be justified within a community of warrant that recognizes no Catholic principle, while (b) demanding that the larger community give points to the Catholics for coming up with the critique that proved of value to the larger community. This proposed trade-off concedes that whatever gives an idea any claim to a distinctly Catholic character is no reason for a larger community to accept that idea, but expects in return that the larger community will continue to recognize the idea's Catholic character.

This move neutralizes the potential of the motivation-warrant distinction to sever from the faith community an idea that promises to enhance the standing of that faith community in the larger world.

This last point invites elaboration. The greater proportion of the inventory of valuable ideas that can be traced to Christianity, the less sense it makes for the prevailing epistemic communities to maintain the critical distance from it that distinguishes them from their counterpart communities of past centuries. Hence there is a tendency to credit religion in general and Christianity in particular with producing and sustaining a host of valuable aspects of contemporary culture, title to which might well be reclaimed, or at least respectfully shared, by other parties. At work here is a familiar dynamic in the struggle for possession of cultural capital. It works as follows.

Ideas the value of which is recognized in a large social arena will be claimed by particular groups as their own contribution. One of the means by which groups achieve, maintain, or lose relative power in a multi-group arena is to be identified or not identified with highly valued items in the common cultural inventory. What endows an item with the capacity to function as cultural capital is the prestige it enjoys among many groups. This dynamic has been especially visible in recent years among ethnoracial groups rather than among religious groups. Consider the following well-known examples. Some Afrocentrists claim the culture of ancient Egypt as the contribution of a descent-community that embraces African Americans of the present day. Some educators have asked that the Iroquois Federation be given credit for having inspired vital aspects of the constitution of the United States. An earlier example is the assertion that democracy is owed to the sturdy Saxons of the primeval German forests who carried it to England and finally to America. Another is Madison Grant's notorious insistence that Jesus Christ belonged not to the Jewish community of descent but to that of the Nordics, by way of the Savior's long-obscured Greek ancestry.

I choose extreme examples to identify the dynamic, not to deny that some claims of this order are true. Indeed, Christianity itself is so massive a presence in the last two millennia that it is not difficult to proliferate credible and convincing claims about how many of the things almost everyone today appreciates came to us through a Christian chain of cultural transferal. The point of understanding the dynamic is not to turn us away from honest inquiries into the historic path by which valuable practices, artifacts, ideals, and doctrines have been created, transferred, preserved, and critically revised. Rather, the point is to be better able to approach critically claims of this kind in a context in which the party making the claims is concerned about its standing in relation to other groups, in this case non-Christian groups. Do we owe Catholicism credit for our colleague's critique of political science? The question needs to be considered in relation to this dynamic.

The need to keep this dynamic in mind is all the more compelling when we see someone assigning to their favorite group credit for cultural commodities that are highly generic. The rule of thumb is this: the more generic the commodity claimed, the more suspect the claim should be. It is common to hear Christianity associated with a set of general virtues, including humility, generosity, decency, charity, and spirituality. Now, Christianity's ordinance has been so large that it is indeed within a Christian context that millions of people have seen the generic virtues articulated and exemplified. When you practice the classic virtues especially well, someone will say, honestly and without artifice, "Oh, you are a good Christian!" When you hear that you are likely to be quite far removed from the faculty club. But I invoke this charming mode of praise to call attention to a presumption that has proved durable even in some academic circles. The presumption is that behaving well and being religious and being Christian are somehow part of the same thing. Another episode from the Lilly Seminar can illustrate this presumption.

One member of the seminar expressed the concern that without the sustaining influence of religious communities, academia was having a hard time transferring "spiritual values" from one generation to the next. This person backed off when he was reminded that lots of non-Christians, even atheists, had proven capable of practicing these virtues as well as Christians could, and even of transferring them to their young. But what I found remarkable was that so able and sensitive a scholar could write and speak as he did in the initial iteration. He was not engaged in a power ploy, I'm sure, but he inherits and sometimes works within a frame of reference that, when it operates in an arena of diverse religious orientations, functions to advance Christianity by reserving to it a unique leadership role in the wholesome project of enabling people to be good.

A closely related incident, this about cosmology rather than ethics, betrayed the same presumption that Christianity owns the title to some very generic cultural material. In this instance, a member of the seminar observed that the knowability of the world and the capacity of humans to grasp parts of its nature were distinctly Christian presuppositions, and that historians, in particular, simply could not do their job effectively without this Christian cosmology. When I asked this colleague if Thucydides and Gibbon and Perry Miller operated on Christian presuppositions despite their lack of Christian commitment, he said yes. Christianity has title, it would seem, to metaphysical and epistemological realism. This view was met with some skepticism in the seminar.

But even many of those who were skeptical about this particular example remained attracted to the basic outlook I have been analyzing here, which can be seen as a fallback position on behalf of the cultural project of Christianity. It is a "fallback" position in the sense that this project, after losing influence over the rules by which truth is established, lays a more adamant claim to being the inspiration, indeed the cultural matrix, out of which arises those truths that do not actually conflict with the project as understood by its current supervisors. Hence there is now so much more talk of Christianity as a set of insufficiently tapped resources, not as a standard for belief. This is another step in the historic process of secularization.

I have been proceeding here in the mode of the "hermeneutics of suspicion," but only for the purposes of bringing out aspects of the conversation on religion and higher education that are often hidden. In concluding, I want to pull back from this mode and call upon my religiously committed colleagues to recognize the virtues of the critical distance mainstream academia now maintains toward Christian commitment. Now that academia is emancipated from a Protestant hegemony, the evils of which surely require no belaboring here, it has proved to be a setting in which Catholics, Protestants, religious Jews, agnostics, atheists, and, more recently Muslims are able to work together in creating good science and scholarship, and in sustaining good teaching programs for graduate and undergraduate students. I believe we should rejoice in this.

Unless we suppose that the religious believers who function well in this environment are somehow less authentic in their faith commitments than those who do not so function, we must surely consider the possibility that the line dividing religious from irreligious scholars is not terribly important, after all, for the purposes of higher education. If it is more important for such purposes—I am not talking about life as a whole, but about higher education—than I grant here, surely our reformers need to provide an analysis of those of their coreligionists who live so successfully within the present system. Is their religion less authentic than that of the reformers?

I sometimes think that our reformers are in the thrall of a parochially Pauline model of religious authenticity. Diaspora Judaism represents an interesting contrasting model, eschewing evangelical modes. And there are other styles of religious commitment and practice. The choice between models of religious authenticity is relevant to teaching as well as to science and scholarship. I am often dismayed at the loose talk about "formation" that I hear from religiously committed colleagues. I wish these colleagues would attend more to the intellectual content of the subject matter they teach, and less to their own conceptions of the moral needs of their students.

Perhaps our reformers need to be reminded that Christianity marched into the modern era as the strongest, most institutionally endowed cultural program in the Western world: Its agents tried through a variety of methods, some more coercive than others, to implant Christian doctrines and practices in as much of the species as possible. Yet as the centuries went forward, this extraordinary presence in world history lost some of the ground it once held. Christianity after the recent end of the century prophesied in 1900 as "the Christian Century" is less triumphant in the North Atlantic West than it was in 1500 or 1700 or 1900. The fate of Protestant culture in the United States is but a fragment of this larger drama of the transformation of the North Atlantic West from a society heavily invested in the cultural program of Christianity to a society in which Christianity found it harder and harder to retain the spiritual capital of its most thoughtful and learned members.

If Christianity's continuing adherents include some of the world's most thoughtful and learned men and women—as I believe they do—let them continue to bear witness as they will. But let's not forget that outside secular academia, Christianity continues to be the cultural norm, not the exception, in the United States. Even today, our society is one in which voters in 2000 could choose between two more-Christian-than-thou presidential candidates: one, George W. Bush, who declared his favorite philosopher to be "Christ," and another, Al Gore, who claimed to solve ethical dilemmas by applying the old formula of Charles Sheldon, "WWJD"(What Would Jesus Do?"). Enough already.

Universities should not surrender back to Christianity the ground they have won for a more independent, cosmopolitan life of the mind. There are plenty of things wrong with higher education in the United States today, but a deficiency in Christianity is not one of them. Of all the parties to our cultural conversation, none has had a greater abundance of opportunities to be heard in the United States than Christianity.

6

The Enlightenment and the Genealogy of Cultural Conflict in the United States

*C*osmopolitanism and the Enlightenment—the connection is axiomatic. Arguments about one often turn into arguments about the other. And nowhere are arguments about cosmopolitanism in recent years more sharp in tone than with reference to the Enlightenment. What makes today's Enlightenment talk so polemical is the decision of so many partisans of conflicting programs for culture to present themselves as either defenders of, or critics of, the Enlightenment.*

Perhaps this extravagant investment in a distant historical episode reflects a lack of confidence about how contemporary intellectual movements should be named, and exactly what is at issue between them? If we are not quite sure where we stand, we can orient ourselves and those with whom we disagree with reference to some abstraction, even one taken from history. This is my suspicion in this case, and it led to this piece.

I argue that the increased eagerness of Anglophone intellectuals since the 1980s to define themselves for or against the Enlightenment owes much to the impulses and initiatives visible under the sign of "postmodernism." Thinkers who described themselves as postmodern, or welcomed this ascription, were often determined to establish their own originality and to distinguish themselves

120

from the merely "modern." But what was the latter? This question was less debated than it was subjected to a variety of not always consistent proclamations. The once common notion that "modernism" was a decidedly post-Enlightenment movement centered in literature and the arts flourishing in the very late nineteenth and early twentieth centuries was jettisoned for a more narrowly French sense that the modern was the Enlightenment itself, especially as embodied in Descartes. It was only the postmodernists, it seems, who were really critical of the Enlightenment. Hence they deserved all the more of our attention.

Historians, oddly enough, have been largely passive while philosophers, literary critics, political theorists, and others have defined the terms on which intellectuals generally have pondered the character and dynamics of the vaunted modern-postmodern divide, and the resulting uncertainties about the nature of the Enlightenment itself. This piece was commissioned for a symposium designed to bring historians together with scholars who appeared to be treating the Enlightenment as a light object, without much historical ballast, that could be moved about by a confident demeanor and a defiant tone. This piece does not provide an answer to Kant's great question, "What is Enlightenment?" But it does try to explain why that question is now proving so difficult to answer.

This essay was published in Keith Michael Baker and Peter Hanns Reill, eds., What's Left of Enlightenment? A Postmodern Question *(Stanford: Stanford University Press, 2001), 8–18, 169–70.*

In 1969, Charlie Manson and his band committed the stylized murders for which they are still remembered. Several months after these grisly events, a faculty colleague of mine at SUNY Buffalo, where he and I had just begun our teaching careers, said to me in a sober voice that if Charlie Manson was what it truly meant to not believe in God—if this cult of murder was the culmination of the historical process of secularization, was what the Enlightenment had come to—he was glad to remain a Christian believer. At first I thought my friend was joking. He was a sophisticated Assistant Professor of English, widely read, and a specialist, as it happened, in the eighteenth century. Surely, he was carrying out the kind of ironic routine that he, as a master of Fielding and Gibbon, of Hume and Johnson, could handle well. But I soon saw he was in earnest, and was trying to send a warning to me, whom he suspected of being rather too far over on the free-thinking side of the spectrum of spiritual orientations. I was non-plussed by my friend's sincerity, and, without thinking, my tongue almost in cheek but not quite, mumbled something to the effect that the Catholicism so dear to him had resulted, after all, in the Spanish Inquisition.

Our friendship somehow survived, for a few years, at least. But I invoke here my memory of this private exchange because its dynamics are similar to many of the public conversations of our own time in which "the Enlightenment" is invoked. It is a discourse of warning and counter-warning, of morally portentous claims and counter-claims, a discourse in which episodes from intellectual history are manipulated and mobilized to discredit or to legitimate one program or another in contemporary struggles. The late Ernest Gellner appears to have believed that his opinions on contemporary issues were endowed with more weight if he identified these opinions with the Enlightenment, and that it discredited his critics to depict them as opponents of the entire body of rational and empirical wisdom built up over the course of two centuries.[1] In the meantime, John Gray seems to think his arguments against certain liberal political theorists are vastly strengthened, and the importance of his own arguments greatly underscored, if it is understood that at issue is the entire heritage of the Enlightenment.[2]

So, on the one side, we are told that the Enlightenment project apotheosized individuality and has left us without means of acting on the elementary communitarian truth that selves are the product of social groups. The Enlightenment project denied the constraints and the enabling consequences of history by assigning to human reason the role of building life anew from a slate wiped clean of tradition. This project tyrannized a host of particular cultural initiatives and tried to make everyone alike by advancing universal rules for identifying goodness, justice, and truth. Politically, the Enlightenment promoted absolutist and imperialist initiatives. Above all, the Enlightenment project blinded us to the uncertainties of knowledge by promoting an ideal of absolute scientific certainty.

Meanwhile, others assure us with equal confidence that the Enlightenment recognized the limits and fallibility of knowledge to a degree that pre-Enlightenment regimes of truth simply did not. This Enlightenment project brought under devastating scrutiny the prejudices and superstitions that protected slavery and a virtual infinity of other injustices. It created the historical and social scientific inquiries that enable us to speak with such confidence about the social dependence of the self. The Enlightenment promoted religious tolerance against the imperialist ambitions of conflicting absolutisms. Above all, the Enlightenment was subversive of traditional political authority, and ultimately it gave us democracy.

Thus we go on merrily, or sometimes grumpily, reenacting Maistre and Mill, just as I played Thomas Jefferson to my Buffalo colleague's Edmund Burke. And while so doing, we add the entire experience of the nineteenth and twentieth centuries to our inventory of historical vehicles that have transported things we like—or don't like—from the eighteenth century to the present. The Enlightenment led to Auschwitz, just as it had led to the Terror; or the Enlightenment led to the principles by which we judge the Terror to have been excessive, just as it led to the standards by which Auschwitz can be the most convincingly condemned today. This dynamic is displayed on shelves of books well beyond the constantly cited works of Lyotard and Habermas, ranging from Alasdair McIntyre's *After Virtue* to Stephen Toulmin's *Cosmopolis,* from Connor Cruise O'Brien's *On the Eve of the Millennium* to John Gray's *Enlightenment's Wake.*[3] I'm hot stuff because I'm not only refuting you, my puny opponent, but I am refuting every great thinker from Descartes to Popper; or, watch out, you think you are arguing against only me, but the implications of your reasoning are to deny the common sense of every humane and rational mind since the seventeenth century. Into such heroic postures we seem to fall into very quickly when we invoke the Enlightenment. One result of this dynamic in some contexts has been to turn the Enlightenment into a conversation-stopper: as soon as one's interlocutor is firmly classified as a defender or a critic of the Enlightenment, a host of associations, loyalties, and counter-loyalties are implicitly in place, and there is little to say.

This is often so in the multiculturalist debates. The Enlightenment is blamed for what is said to be the excessive universalism and individualism that multiculturalists are trying to correct. The Enlightenment, it seems, has led us to suppose that all people are pretty much alike, thus blinding us to diversity. It is another mark of lingering Enlightenment assumptions, moreover, to focus on ostensibly autonomous individuals rather than the groups that provide individuals with their culture. And on the other side of the ideological coin, those who suspect multiculturalism of putting people into a small number of color-coded boxes and expecting them to stay there often voice their complaint in the name of the Enlightenment's revolt against the claims of blood and history. Yet some ideas that might be seen as extensions of an Enlightenment tradition—such as the right of an individual to choose his or her own cultural affiliations regardless of ancestry—are quite acceptable to the same audiences who will be suspicious of these same ideas if they are presented as Enlightenment ideas. A good rule of thumb in the multiculturalist debates is that a good way to get your ideas accepted is to conceal, rather than to emphasize, whatever ancestry those ideas may have in the Enlightenment.[4]

The polemical use of history is common. It would be a mistake to suggest that the case I have described is unique. The legacy of the Enlightenment, in particular, has always been contested because so many enduring religious, political, and philosophical issues were engaged in the historic episode that bears its name. But during the last quarter-century, the Enlightenment has been an extreme case of this dynamic in the United States. Why this has happened is the chief question I pursue here. I want also to comment, more tentatively, on another question: where do we go from here? What are the prospects for an honest inquiry into the long-term historical trajectories in which the Enlightenment-invoking quarrels of our own time are embedded?

An answer to the first question requires an understanding of how the debate over the "modern" was transformed during the 1980s by historical claims offered under the sign of postmodernism. Among Anglophone intellectuals, the term modernism was long used to refer to a cluster of revolts against the Enlightenment. Lionel Trilling's generation used the term "modernism" to refer to Nietzsche, Proust, Conrad, Yeats, Mann, Joyce, Stravinsky, Picasso, Nolde, Klimt, and William James. In a stock-taking essay of 1961, "On the Teaching of Modern Literature," Trilling himself offered a penetrating meditation on the modern canon, commenting on the moral and pedagogical problems presented by each of the texts he used in his legendary course at Columbia University.[5] *Consciousness and Society,* H. Stuart Hughes's a classic work of 1958, considered the social thought of the 1890–1930 epoch largely as a critique of the Enlightenment.[6] The modern canon, in the arts as well as philosophy and social theory, was widely understood in the 1950s and 1960s to be the work of a heroic generation of late-nineteenth- and early-twentieth-century intellectuals who had challenged the epistemological and political traditions of the Enlightenment, and had seen the dark side of what came to be called the modernization process.[7] What had happened during the very late nineteenth and early twentieth centuries, scholars agreed, was a revolt against the positivism, rationalism, realism, and liberalism that the Victorian intellectuals had refined from the Enlightenment of the eighteenth century. Carl Schorske's use of the word "modernism" in his *Fin-de-Siècle*

Vienna of 1980 continued this firmly grounded and widely dispersed historiographical practice.[8]

During the 1980s, however, Anglophone intellectuals attended to a formidable sequence of books and articles that used the word modernism very differently, to refer not to the revolt against the Enlightenment, but to the tradition of the Enlightenment itself. Modernism came to mean not Dostoevsky, but Descartes. Anyone whose sense of modernism had been formed by Richard Ellmann and Charles Feidelson, Jr.'s massive anthology of 1965, *The Modern Tradition,*[9] and by the works of Trilling, Hughes, Schorske, Richard Blackmur, Anthony Quinton, and Irving Howe—to list only some of the most prominent discussants of modernism during the period between 1940 and 1980—had cause to wonder why the term modernism was suddenly being linked with rationalism, the Scientific Revolution, and Kant. These things, one had learned on good authority, were what modernists tried to get beyond.

This new sense of modernism was aggressively retailed in the United States under the name of postmodernism. Nietzsche, after his long career as a founder of modernism, began a new career as a precursor, if not a founder, of postmodernism. The transition can be sometimes found within the work of a single scholar. In 1983 philosopher Robert Pippin described Nietzsche as the prototypical modernist, and in 1991 described Nietzsche as the prototypical postmodernist.[10] Nietzsche's ideas had not changed. Nor had the details of Pippin's analysis of those ideas. The only thing that had changed was the history in which Nietzsche was to be placed, or, more precisely, the movement to which he was assigned. What took place between Pippin's two iterations of Nietzsche's grand historical significance was that modernism had become the Enlightenment and the revolt against it had become postmodernism. The same repackaging was afforded to William James, who, in book after book, made the switch from modernist to postmodernist.

The postmodernists virtually plundered the old modernist canon, appropriating the thinkers they liked for postmodernism and declaring the rest to be lingering echoes of the Enlightenment. In a vivid case of the classic maneuver of appropriation and effacement, some of the postmodernists appropriated the most exciting of the contributions of the canonical modernists and effaced the movement that produced them. The profound tensions within the work of the 1890–1930 generation were relaxed by a new historiography responsive to the hegemonic ambitions of persons who claimed postmodernism as their vehicle. The 1890–1930 historical moment was thus virtually evacuated in order to create a more stark and momentous confrontation between postmodernism and the old Enlightenment of Descartes and Kant. There was virtually nothing of consequence in between. Hardly anybody, it seemed, had really seen through the illusions of the Enlightenment until the postmodernists came along. All those folks who thought everything had changed on or about December 1910 were kidding themselves. There was a big break, all right, but it did not take place in Bloomsbury on the eve of World War I. It took place in Paris after 1968. One book after another carrying postmodernism in its title provided a capsule history of postmodernism, in which the generation of 1890–1930 was treated not as the group of heroic, agonistic explorers whose careers had been analyzed by Trilling and Howe, by Hughes and Schorske, but as a pusillanimous prolegomenon to Foucault.[11]

Entailed in this transformation in the Enlightenment's relation to modernism was the more widespread acceptance, by American academics, of a notion of intellectual modernity that had been popular in France, and that achieved currency in the United States along with the ideas of French theorists whose names were associated with postmodernism.[12] Two autonomous revolts against two quite distinctive modernisms merged, apparently without anyone's planning it or negotiating it.[13] The first modernism was that taken for granted when the term postmodernism was first invoked by Leslie Fiedler, Susan Sontag, and Howe in the United States in the 1960s. The modernism against which these writers and their American contemporaries defined postmodernism was still the modernism of Eliot and Pound and Nietzsche and James; this was the modernism that entailed a critique of the Enlightenment and of the social and cultural processes of "modernization." Fiedler and Sontag and others thought this old modernism, as appreciated in the pages of the *Partisan Review* and the *Hudson Review*, had become academicized and stuffy. In this context, postmodernism seemed a refreshing change. It was found in the fiction of Thomas Pynchon and the music of John Cage. But a resoundingly different version of modernism, one associated with the Enlightenment, was the counter-referent for Lyotard's *Postmodern Condition*, translated into English in 1984.[14] The French conversation that produced Lyotard had been preoccupied, moreover, not with the arts, but with ideas about language, power, and the human subject that had been developed by philosophers, psychologists, and political theorists.

The authority of this French-centered conversation was facilitated by several specific features of the American intellectual scene. Active engagement with Lyotard was encouraged in the mid-80s by the antiphilosophical philosopher Richard Rorty, who briefly but portentously took for himself the label postmodernist and began to write about Proust and Nabokov shortly after having revived a pragmatic antifoundationalism for which the way had been prepared by Thomas S. Kuhn. These literary-philosophical explorations of Rorty's — grounded in James, Dewey, and Kuhn, and openly appreciative of the political tradition of American liberalism — served to enlarge and extend the postmodernist debate in the United States.[15] Another engagement was manifest in the work of Frederic Jameson, the most influential Marxist literary critic of the era. Jameson's critical studies of canonical modernists preceded his widely discussed paper of 1984, "Postmodernism, or the Cultural Logic of Late Capitalism," which addressed many genres of modernism and of postmodernism.[16] Simultaneously, Jürgen Habermas' attacks on the French postmodernists and on Hans-Georg Gadamer for betraying the Enlightenment project invited the large contingent of American followers of the Frankfurt School to engage the issues, and of course to see postmodernism's modernism as that of the Enlightenment.

Still, these two quite distinctive postmodernisms—an American, literary-artistic postmodernism defined against the canonical modernists of 1890–1930, and a French, philosophical-political postmodernism defined against the Enlightenment—might not have become part of the same discourse were it not for the quaint belief that there is but a single torch to be passed, requiring that each moment in the discourse of intellectuals be named. What is our moment? Why, the moment of postmodernism, of course. How do we know what it is? Well, we can start by scrutinizing the various things said and done under its sign. By the end of the 1980s the Anglophone world was awash with sweeping assessments of architecture, poetry, film, social theory, epistemology, fiction, and political economy, all of which were said to partake of postmodernism in the French sense of the term.[17] Older critiques of the Enlightenment that had previously attained only a tiny constituency, such as Theodor Adorno and Max Horkheimer's *Dialectic of Enlightenment*, a book published in German in the 1940s but translated into English only in 1972, gained unprecedented currency.[18]

Hence the Enlightenment made the historic transition from a distant episode long interrogated by the great modernists into a vibrant enemy of the newest and most exciting insights coming from Paris. The Enlightenment was dehistoricized, and made into a vivid and somewhat dangerous presence insufficiently criticized and transcended by previous generations of intellectuals. It was up to us, now in the 1980s and 1990s, to do the job right, to complete the anti-Enlightenment project. No wonder the tensions surrounding the name of the Enlightenment sharply increased. All of

the historic layers of mediation between "us" and the Enlightenment had been put aside. The Enlightenment became more relevant to contemporary cultural conflicts because the discourse of
postmodernism made it so.

Where do we go from here? One response to the ease with which
discursive blacksmiths forge and shatter links between ourselves
and the Enlightenment is to suspend, temporarily, at least, explicit
assertions of the Enlightenment or counter-Enlightenment significance of contemporary debates. If the Enlightenment can be
moved around so easily to suit contemporary doctrinal agendas,
perhaps it is not worth the struggle to establish a warranted account of the Enlightenment and its consequences. We might be
better off with a more relaxed attitude toward the Enlightenment,
and toward history in general, accompanied by a determination
to formulate contemporary issues in terms that are closer to the
ground. New openings and new alliances might come about in
contemporary debates if the partisans are less determined to
identify their own positions with symbolically charged discursive
giants of the past. Simultaneously, we might rehistoricize the Enlightenment with a vengeance. A stronger historiography of the
Enlightenment might emerge from a conviction that eighteenth-
century studies can flourish well enough without exaggerated
claims to relevance in contemporary culture wars. Enlightenment
studies might then become more like patristics and Tang sinology,
worthy *Wissenschafte* whose findings are relatively removed from
debates over the character and direction of our civilization.

Yet this approach, tempting as it will be to anyone who has
encountered the Enlightenment in its capacity as a conversation-
stopper, runs into difficulties when enacted. Consider what happens when we try this in relation to a set of ideas that were widely
adhered to by American intellectuals in the 1940s and 1950s, were
then brought under severe suspicion at one point or other between the late 1960s and the 1980s, and have more recently been

subject to critical revision and reassertion. Before I list some of the ideas that fall into this class, let me underscore the distinctive historical destiny of these ideas. This class is quite specific; it does not include ideas that were bequeathed by the World War II generation yet were not called sharply into question by the next generation. Excluded, also, are ideas that were so bequeathed and then so challenged yet were not reasserted with noteworthy vigor. I call attention only to ideas that underwent all three experiences: popular in the 1940s and 1950s, then subject to widespread suspicion, and, finally, subject to critical reformulation and defense in recent years. Such ideas—argued about so earnestly, and subject to sharp reversals—are obviously important to the intellectual life of our own time. Any study of American intellectual life since 1950 needs an analytic language for interpreting these ideas.

What ideas fall into this distinctive class? Let me suggest seven, although the list could no doubt be extended:

> Nature has a capacity to significantly resist or respond to human efforts to represent it and to intervene in it.
> Humankind as a whole is a valid epistemic unit.
> Intersubjective reason has great emancipatory potential.
> Civil liberties formulated on the basis of rights ascribed to individual citizens are indispensable to a just society.
> Religion, whatever its role in past centuries, is now likely to be irrelevant, or even an obstruction, to cognitive and social progress.
> Physical characteristics such as skin color and shape of the face should not be allowed to determine the cultural tastes and social associations of individuals.
> The United States is potentially a world-historical agent of democratic-egalitarian values.

These ideas were affirmed with conviction by a great variety of voices during the 1940s and 1950s, when modernization theorists and positivists and behaviorists and liberals and integrationists of many kinds were in vogue: the Walt Rostows and the Hans Reichenbachs, the Perry Millers and the David Trumans, the Gunnar

Myrdals and Cary McWilliamses of those years. Each of the seven was later brought under suspicion, often by persons identified with one or more of the following movements: communitarianism, feminism, neoconservatism, poststructuralism, Marxism, postmodernism, and multiculturalism. These seven ideas are now situated in the classic baby-and-bathwater domain. Some say, in effect, "forget it, it's time we got beyond those ideas, let's talk about something else," and other people respond, "wait a minute, there's something here we can probably still use, if we are careful about it." And some who say "forget it" concerning one or another of the seven will switch sides about another of the seven, and say, "hold on, I like that one if we can make it non-racist, non-sexist, non-imperialist, non-universalist, non-logocentric, non-formalist, and, above all, non-European."

Accepting one of these ideas does not require one to accept the others. One of our most indefatigable skeptics about the epistemic unity of all humankind, about the capacity of nature to provide non-discursive restraints upon our representations of it, and about the emancipatory potential of intersubjective reason is at the same time a notorious defender of the American nation-state as an instrument for democratic-egalitarian values, and a scourge of the religiosity found in the likes of Stephen Carter and Christopher Lasch. I refer to Richard Rorty.

Each of the seven ideas on my little list deserves its own history within the discourse of the American academic intelligentsia since 1950. I invoke these ideas here only to render concrete the challenge of dealing with recent intellectual history in relation to the question of the Enlightenment's legacy. Are these seven ideas "Enlightenment ideas"? Of what significance is it that one thinker who accepted all of them—Ernest Gellner—called himself an "Enlightenment Rationalist Fundamentalist"?[19] Is Anthony Appiah a "neo-Enlightenment thinker" by virtue of his defense of cosmopolitanism?[20] Is Ian Hacking, by virtue of his critique of popular notions of "social construction"?[21] Is Michael Ignatieff, by virtue of his perspective on "blood and belonging"?[22] Does the critical revision and reassertion of these ideas in very recent years amount to a "neo-Enlightenment" of sorts? I state these questions not to answer them, but to suggest that if one wants to be historical at all, it is difficult to analyze some central feature of recent American intellectual life without making at least some use of the Enlightenment. The universalism and individualism prominent in the list surely owe much to Christianity, but so does the Enlightenment itself. The potential connection between the Enlightenment and these seven energetic ideas of our own time cannot be disposed of simply by pointing to a "more complicated" intellectual ancestry. At issue, rather, is whether we can get very far in explaining how these ideas have come to us, and how they acquired the hold they have on our conversations, without making extensive use of the collection of seventeenth- and eighteenth-century-centered episodes that we continue to call "the Enlightenment."

This is to suggest that if we are going to make any use at all of intellectual history in trying to understand where we are today, the Enlightenment is extremely difficult to avoid. The temptation to turn away in disgust and frustration at the polemicism of recent uses of the Enlightenment should be resisted. To give in to this temptation would be to deny our own historicity, and to shrink from searching for the sources and sustaining conditions of the ideas that animate much of contemporary intellectual life. We might save the Enlightenment from polemicism, but at a considerable cost: we might cut off too abruptly an opportunity for the cultural self-knowledge that history is supposedly in the business of providing. Historians have been relatively passive in the disputes in which the Enlightenment has been invoked; rather, the thinkers who have been most active in those disputes are philosophers, literary scholars, and political theorists. Historians have put remarkably little resistance—in venues where it counts—to the transformation of modernism from Dostoevsky to Descartes, and to the proliferation of cardboard-character representations of the Enlightenment mind.

Facing and trying to bring reason and evidence to the polemics that invoke episodes from intellectual history, then, comes with the intellectual historian's calling unless one simply wants to withdraw from the concerns of one's colleagues in other parts of the humanities and social sciences. We should not shy away from constructing the most historically sound Enlightenment we can, and from offering the best arguments we can about its consequences. If someone claims, as did the author of a recent book, *Hitler as Philosophe,* that Hitler was a follower of Rousseau on sexuality and of Ricardo on economics, that he was a Jacobin in his religious orientation, and that he was, in general, a popularizer—in the words of the *American Historical Review*'s reviewer—of "Enlightenment values" such as "optimism, progress, and human perfectibility through adherence to natural law,"[23] these claims should be confronted head-on.

This requires that those of us who work primarily in the history of the twentieth century listen to what our colleagues in Enlightenment studies have to say. I hope we can count on our colleagues in seventeenth- and eighteenth-century studies to provide us with a sound and stable sense of the Enlightenment to work with. But you never know what they will say. In a recent issue of *Critical Inquiry,* one scholar argued that the true Enlightenment, the complete Enlightenment, the one expression of the Enlightenment that did not deny its own ferocious imperative for truth, was found not in Kant, not in Rousseau, not in Locke. The complete Enlightenment, this scholar explained, was found in that most commanding of all efforts to integrate power and knowledge, the Spanish Inquisition.[24] If my Buffalo friend had understood this in 1969, he could have had the last laugh on me.

7

Why are Jews Preeminent in Science and Scholarship?

The Veblen Thesis Reconsidered

*T*he *"cosmopolitan Jew" is a stereotypical character in the drama of modern history, a figure sometimes seen as a threat to this or that provincial culture's "home truths," but in other contexts seen as wholesome explorer of a wider and wider world. Among the soundest bases for the stereotype is the remarkable demographic overrepresentation of Jews in the international communities of science and scholarship. Just why there are so many Jews among Nobel Prize winners and elsewhere in the ranks of leading intellectuals is a puzzle of long standing. One of the most influential attempts to solve this puzzle was made in 1919 by the American social theorist, Thorstein Veblen. The piece below is an appraisal of Veblen's thesis from today's perspective.*

Veblen's thesis focused on the social location of Jewish intellectuals between two solidarities. When Jews departed from the traditional Jewish community, hoping for acceptance within gentile communities, they were often rebuffed by gentiles. The resulting rootlessness endowed Jews, Veblen argued, with virtues of detachment and disinterestedness that Veblen believed conducive to intellectual achievement. But this thesis actually explains very little, and begs a host of questions it raises. I argue that Veblen's extravagant admiration for a sensibility of alienation and his almost fanatical antipathy for commercial pursuits blinded him to a number of facets of Jewish history that could help solve the puzzle. I argue, further, that we need a demystified approach to the study of Jewish overrepresentation, according to which we would analyze Jewish intellectual preeminence alongside, rather than in isolation from, Jewish preeminence in many other callings, including the arts, the service professions, and finance.

Some readers who found my critique of the Veblen thesis sound, and who were convinced by my account of how and why Veblen came to the conclusions that he did, complained that I stopped short. What might a good, demystified answer to the puzzle of Jewish preeminence look like? Under such prodding I pushed the envelope a bit farther in the piece I reprint in this volume following this discussion of Veblen. Hence this essay and the piece following it are best read as a pair.

This essay was first published in Aleph II *(2002): 145–63.*

Why were one-third of the German citizens who won Nobel Prizes between 1901 and 1940 born into that tiny fraction of the German population that was of Jewish descent? Why have Jews been demographically overrepresented by factors of six and even ten or twelve in departments of the leading universities of the United States in the second half of the twentieth century?

Questions like these often lead to Thorstein Veblen, the most creative American social theorist of the early twentieth century. In 1919, twenty years after he published his most famous work, *The Theory of the Leisure Class*, this Wisconsin-born son of Norwegian immigrants wrote "The Intellectual Preeminence of Jews in Modern Europe."[1] At that time, the drift of gentile opinion was in a decidedly anti-Semitic direction. Quotas were being introduced to limit Jewish enrollment in colleges and universities, and editorial attacks on the Russian Revolution called portentous attention to the fact that many of the leading Bolsheviks were Jews. But Veblen, like such Anglo-Protestant contemporaries as Randolph Bourne and Hutchins Hapgood, was enthralled by the Jews he met on the Lower East Side of New York City. Veblen went against the anti-Semitic tide. His essay was one of the most adamantly philosemitic treatises ever written by a gentile. After more than eighty years, it remains the most influential analysis of Jewish intellectual creativity.

Veblen's answer to the question of Jewish overrepresentation in the ranks of leading scientists and scholars centered on the partial liberation of Jews from traditional Judaism and Jewish communal life. This liberation in itself yields a skeptical temper, Veblen explained, which is then reinforced by the refusal of gentile society to altogether welcome the Jew. The combination of withdrawal from Jewish tradition and only partial assimilation into gentile society endows the intellectual Jew with the virtue of detachment. Skeptical, estranged, alienated, the liberated Jew, as Veblen described this distinctive character in the drama of modern European history, was ideally suited for a career of science and scholarship. This marginal man, this "wanderer in the intellectual no-man's land," could see "unmediated facts" that were less readily observed by minds still clouded by Judaism, Christianity, local customs, tribal idols, or other premodern frames of reference

This is the Veblen thesis. Veblen scholars have long agreed that, whatever its plausibility, the motives behind the Veblen thesis were strongly personal. This legendary essay was Veblen's most vividly etched self-portrait. Veblen developed the apotheosis of alienation into an art form, and nowhere did he practice this art more skillfully than in this essay, in which he projected his alienated self onto Jewish intellectuals.

The projection was credible. Marx, Freud, Durkheim, and Einstein were emancipated, freethinking Jews. Although Veblen mentioned none of them explicitly, reference to these four names can alert us that we do not have to look far in the intellectual history of the nineteenth and twentieth centuries to find, at the very apex of *wissenschaftliche* creativity, individuals to whom it is at least plausible to apply Veblen's terms. Veblen's thesis was engaged with great sympathy by Seymour Martin Lipset and Everett Carll Ladd, Jr., in the most sustained and empirically grounded effort yet made to address the intellectual presence of Jews in American academic life since the Second World War.[2] More recently, Paul Mendes-Flohr, in one of the most methodologically rigorous explorations of Jewish intellectual achievement ever written, was drawn back to Veblen when one possible explanation after another lost credibility under his close scrutiny.[3]

One reason for the popularity of the Veblen thesis is that it purports to explain, not simply intelligence, but something more specific: the successful use of intelligence in science and scholarship, in the rigorous, methodical study of the world. Veblen does not address the question of whether Jews are somehow smarter than other people. Has the Catholic practice of priestly celibacy denied the Christian population of the West the strong intellectual inheritance said to have been provided by the Jewish practice of encouraging rabbis to marry and reproduce? Versions of this biocentric explanation for the perceived intelligence of Jews have been put forth often. But the Veblen thesis has no role for genes.

Veblen was not interested in who might prove to be good at playing chess or composing string quartets or writing poems, or getting the best of a commercial rival or any number of other human activities that demand intelligence. No doubt basic smartness has a lot to do with winning Westinghouse science competitions in high school and Nobel prizes in maturity; perhaps much more than Veblen supposed. But Veblen's own contribution, for whatever it may be worth, was not to explain intelligence. Rather, Veblen singled out a specific intellectual style, a habit of thought that he believed enabled one to have a better perception of the world as it is, and tried to show why Jews were more likely than other people to have this style. Those who have been curious about the fact of Jewish preeminence in science and scholarship, then, have found in Veblen a theorist who focuses exactly on that issue but without asserting that Jews are smarter than Asante or

Armenians or Nubians or Norwegians or Chinese or Cherokees. Those who want to establish a hierarchy of ethnoracial groups by intelligence will get no help from Veblen.

But how much help does Veblen provide to people pursuing nongenetic inquiries? Can the Veblen thesis be applied to the case of the United States in the period after Veblen wrote, especially since the Second World War? In pursuing these questions, I will not be developing and defending a comprehensive answer to the question of Jewish preeminence in science and scholarship. My purpose is more modest. I will review the circumstances that keep the question alive. I will bring to bear on the discussion of this question several considerations that Veblen ignored and some that have become more relevant during the decades since he wrote. I will plead for an approach more fully historical than Veblen's. And I will insist that we merge the question of Jewish achievement in science and scholarship with that of Jewish achievement in other fields.

The American case since the Second World War demands attention because historians agree that the flourishing of Jews in this setting is unique in the history of the Diaspora. And the transformation of Jews from victimized outsiders to leaders of the American intellectual establishment took place in the course of a single generation. Before the war, Jews were systematically discriminated against in the hiring practices of many universities. It was not until 1946, for example, that the first Jew was appointed to a professorship in Yale College, the culturally strategic core of Yale University. But by 1970, only twenty-four years later, 18 percent of Yale College faculty holding the rank of professor were Jewish, as were 22 percent of those holding this rank in the University as a whole (so were the deans of seven of the University's ten schools and colleges in 1967).[4]

The historical forces that lowered the barriers against Jews included the discrediting of anti-Semitism by the Nazis and the development of a Cold War that divided the world, ostensibly, by ideology rather than by ethnoracial groups. The process by which elite academia became open to Jews is a complicated and interesting story in itself. Here I simply want to call attention to the magnitude of the change that followed the lowering of anti-Jewish barriers. In our era of conspicuously declared and monitored identities, when the relative destiny of communities of descent has been a matter of intense public concern, surprisingly little attention has been paid to this remarkable case of overrepresentation. Yet it is the most dramatic single case in all of American history in which a stigmatized ethnoracial group, which had been the victim of systematic and legal discrimination, suddenly became astonishingly overrepresented and even more suddenly ceased to be counted as a group relevant to the whole calculus of group representation.

In 1969, the year for which we have the most reliable data (thanks to a Carnegie Commission study designed by Martin Trow), 17 percent of the tenure and tenure-track faculty in the nation's most prestigious universities identified themselves as Jewish. But this figure included departments of agriculture and physical education, where there were almost no Jewish faculty members. The data by discipline was more informative. The Carnegie study found that 26 percent of the combined physics departments of these universities identified themselves as Jewish, as did 28 percent of the economists. Other figures by discipline, included 20 percent for philosophers, 22 percent for historians, 34 percent for sociologists, and 36 percent for professors of law. Hence Jews, whom demographers said constituted about 3 percent of the population of the United States at the time, were overrepresented in elite academia as a whole by a factor of nearly six, in physics by a factor of nearly nine, and in legal scholarship by a factor of twelve.[5]

How much light can the Veblen thesis cast on these figures? A little, I think, but not as much as has often been supposed. Let me explain some deficiencies of the Veblen thesis that are made especially evident when we have the case of the modern United States in mind.

Veblen flattens the long-term history of Jewish-gentile relations by treating the entirety of the Diaspora, from ancient times to the origins of the Zionist movement, as a single sociological piece. He ignores altogether the unique force of the Haskalah, the great Jewish enlightenment that flowered in the eighteenth and especially the nineteenth centuries. Changed policies in Russia, the Habsburg domains, and other states created unprecedented opportunities for Jews to follow Spinoza and Mendelssohn, and the Marranos of Spain and Portugal, in confronting the science and secular learning of gentile Europe on its own terms. These are the circumstances that seem to have produced so many examples of the cultural type that inspired Veblen: the skeptical intellectual poised between contrasting, and to some extent competing, modes of thought and feeling. What Veblen missed was the historical particularity of the moment when the traditional Jewish respect for learning came face-to-face, all at once, with the Renaissance, the Scientific Revolution, and the Enlightenment. This explosive historical moment was closer to Marx, Freud, Durkheim, and Einstein than it was to post-1945 American life, but it is reasonable to suppose that this last, too, was affected by its legacy. Many of the Jews who became prominent in science and scholarship in the middle decades of the twentieth century were the children and grandchildren of immigrants who had experienced the Haskalah at first hand. Veblen prided himself on his attention to the dynamics of history, but in this case he posited a virtually timeless tension between Jewish and gentile society that blinded him to changes that a more vigorously historical explanation would want to take into account.

The highly abstract character of Veblen's history is matched by the abstractness of his notion of the intellectual Jew. Although Veblen is often felt to have been bold for 1919 in emphasizing the "hybridity" of intellectual Jews, once he acknowledged this hybridity Veblen treated the liberated Jewish mind monolithically, as possessed of a single and stable set of traits and dispositions derived from an enduring dynamic of Jewish-gentile relations.

Today, we might accuse Veblen of "essentialism"—of ascribing to all Jewish intellectuals a particular orientation that persists through all historical circumstances and remains a defining element even in the most emancipated of apostates. This failure to acknowledge the internal diversity of the population of Jewish intellectuals is problem enough for comprehending the situation in 1919. But it is even more of a problem with reference to the post-1945 United States. To study Jewish intellectuals prominent in American science and scholarship in that setting, we need to proceed in an anti-essentialist fashion. This is in keeping with the welcome new emphasis, in ethnic studies, on the internal diversity of groups and on the contingent and historically specific character of the culture that ethnoracially defined communities present to the larger society at any given moment. Some Jews came directly from Hitler's Europe, others were the children of East European immigrants from the 1880–1924 era of mass migration, and still others were the descendants of German Jews who had come to the United States before 1880. Some were religiously orthodox and others had no use for Judaism; some passed as gentiles while others articulated and commented upon Jewish subjectivity. Some came to maturity when anti-Jewish quotas were in place and others at a time when such quotas were a remote memory.

Recognition of this internal diversity of the relevant population of Jewish intellectuals can help us view another feature of Veblen's analysis skeptically. Veblen's mystification of alienation, marginality, and homelessness is highly suspect and deflects our vision from other syndromes manifest in the lives of some Jews. Veblen was so enamored of the persona of the detached critic that he gave short shrift to the possibility that a sustaining social community, with a coherent culture, might promote rather than retard intellectual creativity. This is not to question that Veblen was on to something, but it does caution against an uncritical acceptance of Veblen's implication that communities are more often obstacles than facilitators. In our multiculturalist era, the enabling, rather than the disabling, functions of ethnoracially defined communities are everywhere affirmed. No doubt this emphasis on the value of tightly knit ethnic communities has been overdone in some contexts. But we must surely be alert for signs Veblen might have missed that Jewish communal life promoted intellect, even in the form of psychological capital carried by certain families and individuals who were one, two, or even more generations removed from that communal life.

That psychological capital is difficult to measure, but it is not unreasonable to suppose that some of it has been distributed even to the most assimilated of American Jews. Jewish social solidarity has a long history, perpetuated by external persecution as well as by internal religious adhesives, Veblen's refusal to explore even tentatively the specific cultural and social history of Diaspora Jewry limits Veblen's utility as a starting point for any analysis of the history of Jewish intellectuals.

Consider, for example, one obvious part of that cultural and social history: the extraordinarily high rate of literacy within Diaspora Jewry. This is a formidably relevant point, but Veblen makes nothing of it. A comparative analysis of the intellectual contributions made by members of various groups could no doubt go far simply by treating the literacy rate as a social-scientific predictor of *wissenschaftliche* activities and attainments. Literacy as such may simply beg the question—what explains the differential rates of literacy from one people to another? But Veblen's failure to confront so obvious a potential factor, and the obvious role of rabbinical Judaism in promoting literacy, is one of the surprising features of his essay.

Another surprising omission from Veblen's analysis is the distinctively universalist epistemic ideal associated with science. Jews had some reason to hope that the quest for truth about nature was one arena of human striving in which their contributions would be evaluated fairly, rather than on an ethnoracially biased scale. This suggests that some of the success of Jews in science and scholarship might derive from the exceptional amount of energy devoted to that calling by people who believed that there, at least, their work would be received with a minimum of prejudice.

Yet the most surprising single property of Veblen's text, when we read it afresh today, is its silence about the economic activities and economic position of Jews. This silence might be construed as all to the good, insofar as it entails a refusal on Veblen's part to accommodate and reinforce anti-Jewish stereotypes. The era's greatest scourge of the pecuniary withheld his fire when he spoke about Jews. Veblen's essay of 1919 is in no way a Jewish postscript to his slashing book of twenty years earlier, *The Theory of the Leisure Class*. The wealthy parasites of Veblen's most enduring work, those exemplars of conspicuous consumption who seduce the masses from virtuous industry, those predatory barbarians, are not Jewish. If we emancipate ourselves from Veblen's ferociously anti-commercial bias and are willing to explore his question about Jews in the economic matrix that he himself emphasized in most of his other work, we find a welcome opportunity to demystify the entire question of the preeminence of Jews in science and scholarship. Had Veblen been less hostile to commercial culture and less determined to employ Jewish intellectuals as counter-models to it, he might have explored the possible relevance to his inquiry of the class position of Jews.

The most recent list of the wealthiest Americans reported that 40 percent were of Jewish descent. Interestingly, this correlates exactly with the percentage of Jews among the American winners of Nobel Prizes during the last thirty years and with the percentage of Jewish partners in the leading law firms in New York and Washington: both are also 40 percent. Not all the relevant statistics follow the marvelous consistency of these figures, which I take from the recent book, *Jews and the New American Scene*, by Lipset and Earl Raab.[6] But the strong class position of Jews is beyond dispute. When the demographically disproportionate attainments of Jews in science and scholarship is placed alongside the demographically disproportionate attainments of Jews in the liberal professions, business, and finance, Jewish intellectual preeminence invites explanations that explain these other instances of Jewish preeminence as well. Even if detachment and alienation are assumed to be good qualifications for a career in science, they may not be necessary for success as a Hollywood producer or an investment banker. Strong class position does not necessarily foster intellectual achievement, but our sociologists are constantly reminding us that it can certainly help. If weak class position helps explain the underrepresentation of African Americans and Hispano-Americans in the leadership of American science and scholarship, as we are so often told, then doesn't strong class position tell us more than the Veblen thesis does about what groups are overrepresented?

Yet most of the Jews who immigrated to the United States between 1880 and 1924 were poor. An economically centered interpretation of the destiny of Jews in twentieth-century America, it might be said, begs the question. Jews may have attained strong class position by the middle decades of the century; but look at the situation in 1900 or 1910, when the Lower East Side of New York was filled with laborers. What needs to be added is that many of the poor Jews of the great migration from the Russian Empire had been only recently proletarianized on a large scale. Many had been driven out of their traditional occupations as artisans and small traders. These impoverished Eastern European Jewish immigrants were, as Nathan Glazer pointed out long ago, often "the sons or the grandsons of merchants and scholars." They were not, like most of the non-Jewish workers who immigrated with them from the same societies in 1890 and 1910, "the sons of workers and peasants, bearing the traditionally limited horizons of those classes." Business and education were not remote for these Jewish immigrants; many Jews were fully possessed of a middle-class culture created by generations of commercial activity and were thus able to respond to the social and economic conditions in the United States in the era of the great migration.[7]

Comfortable class position frequently facilitates creativity not only in science and scholarship, but also in the arts. Veblen said nothing about artistic creativity. Yet if we look at the ethnoreligious demography of music and painting and sculpture and of course fiction and poetry (to say nothing of film) in the United States since 1945, we encounter a panorama of achievement by artists of Jewish descent on which Veblen's analysis sheds very little light. One could argue that detachment, alienation, and skepticism foster artistic creativity too, thus expanding and perhaps saving the Veblen thesis. But Veblen himself did not expand his argument in that direction.

Uncertainty about the scope of human activities facilitated by detachment, alienation, and skepticism prompts closer scrutiny of the claim, made by Veblen and many others, that science is peculiarly facilitated by these qualities. Is Veblen so obviously right about this? Might a certain drive to belong, even to conform, be just as vital to success in a tightly organized scientific community as is a stance of critical detachment? Veblen wrote long before Thomas Kuhn made us aware of what the latter once called the function of dogma in science. But even apart from what we learn from Kuhn in particular, today's understandings of how scientific communities work render Veblen's portrait of the scientific personality as highly independent and detached at least mildly suspect. If success in science often entails getting along with an organization, perhaps Veblen's terms need to be turned around?

This is exactly the implication of some recent work by the Israeli historian, Shulamit Volkov. In the most careful empirical study to date of leading Jewish and non-Jewish physical and biological scientists in modern Germany, Volkov finds that the most successful of the Jewish scientists were anything but Vebleneseque skeptics. In an earlier study, Volkov had quoted Freud's famous remark that seems to support Veblen's thesis: "Because I was a Jew," Freud wrote, "I found myself free of many prejudices, which restrict others in the use of the intellect. As a Jew, I was prepared to be in opposition and to give up agreement with the 'compact major-ity.'" This was not true of Jewish physical and biological scientists in late-nineteenth- and early-twentieth-century Germany, Volkov insists. Most of the Jewish scientists who attained distinction "were conventional, orderly people, basically seeking to conform—both in their socio-political attitudes and in their scientific practice," she writes. Einstein is almost unique among them in fitting the Veblen-Freud model. It is the careers of several leading non-Jewish scien-tists, especially Wilhelm Roentgen and F. W. Ostwald, that Volkov sees as exemplifying the Veblenesque persona of the detached skeptic, the opposite of the conformist, paradigm-confirming men-tality. If there was a path to scientific eminence in Germany that was followed more by Jews than by non-Jews, that path, accord-ing to Volkov, was affirming convention, working within, rather than against, the social and epistemic expectations of the powers that be.[8]

Volkov's study encourages the speculation that Veblen got marginality wrong and that the theorists who got it right are those who argue, contra Veblen, that marginality breeds a desire to con-form. The marginality experienced by Jews may have had the ef-fect, at least in some circumstances, not of rendering Jews more distant from the conventional wisdom of their social and epi-stemic communities, not more liberated from their prejudices, but more determined to win approval within those communities and more accepting of their norms. In this view, marginality propelled Jews to succeed through the mentality of hyper-belonging rather than through hyper-detachment.

Now, it is possible that Volkov's testing of the Veblen thesis is too literal minded. She may downplay the possibility that Jews in the scientific world of Imperial Germany owed some of their creativity to a Veblenesque persona that they largely concealed in the interests of refuting the image of the Jew as subversive. And what she found for the physical and biological scientists of the *Kaiserreich* may not apply to other times and places, such as the

United States, especially after 1945. Even were Volkov's results to be reproduced in studies of physical and biological scientists in the United States or Russia or England, moreover, those results would leave open the possibility that Veblen's thesis still applies to other *wissenschaftliche* callings, such as the social sciences—the home, after all, of Marx, Freud, Durkheim, Franz Boas, and the American sociologists surveyed by the Carnegie investigators in 1969. But Volkov's work is an extremely valuable corrective against the facile use of Jews and of science itself as instruments in the celebration of critical detachment. Veblen was a skeptic before and after he discovered Jews and projected himself upon them. It is no disrespect to Veblen, or to Jews, or to science, or even to critical detachment to suggest that neither Jews nor science was quite so firm a foundation for Veblen's cultural program as he supposed.

If Veblen took it too much for granted that social marginality produced detachment and that detachment produced good science, he also took too it too much for granted that history would constantly repeat itself. Veblen asserted that Jews were "forever" destined to be pariahs when in gentile society and to be complacently self-absorbed when gathered in their own tribe. I have not studied the intellectual history of Israel since 1948, but I suspect it would provide some grounds for questioning Veblen's notion that any triumph of Zionism would produce an intellectual "life of complacent futility." And the recent history of Jews in the United States surely gives reason to treat as anachronistic Veblen's claim that "the most genial share in the gentile community's life" likely to befall a Jew "is that of being interned."[9] One wonders what Veblen would make of the earnest contemporary debate surrounding the suspicion that the survival of the Jewish people has been placed at risk by emancipation, the diminution of prejudice, and the extent of assimilation many American Jews find possible and desirable. An America in which perhaps half of the marriages involving Jews entail the acquisition of a gentile spouse is a society altogether beyond the limits of Veblen's vision, which entertained no possibility of change.

Beyond the limits of Veblen's vision, too, is the formation of a transethnic community of intellectuals for which the liberated Jew of Veblen's idealized description was a model. As Milton Gordon and others have observed, something very much like this happened in American academia during the middle decades of the twentieth century. The "real melting pot in American life," according to Gordon, is the academic and literary arenas, where there has emerged a "subsociety of intellectuals" that holds itself apart from the nation as a whole, rather in the manner of a traditional ethnic group.[10]

The vitality of this transethnic intelligentsia and the frequency of intermarriage and reproduction across ethnoracial lines has made the United States a rather different society for Jews than those that are most often invoked when inquiries are made into the intellectual preeminence of Jews. The United States is also made different by its ethnoracially plural character. A variety of European communities of descent, as well as those derived from Africa, Asia, South America, and North America itself, have produced a discourse about assimilation and group identity very different from those in Britain, Italy, France, Germany, the Netherlands, and most other countries. In those places, Jews as a group were defined in the classic way, primarily in relation to a single, "host" group with a long-standing proprietorship of the state and its geographical territory. Yet in the United States, Jewish identity came to be considered in the context of African American, Italian American, Irish American, Japanese American and other identities, the contingent character of which became apparent by the 1980s, when Jews were absorbed, for many purposes, into an amorphous "European American" identity. The presence of these other groups is a crucial aspect of the Jewish experience in modern America, not always grasped by those who have considered issues in Jewish assimilation largely through an interpretive paradigm generated by the cases of Germany, France, Italy, Poland, and Great Britain. Veblen operated within such an interpretive paradigm, as have most other discussants of Jewish intellectual achievement. Yet in America, the public meaning of being Jewish has come increasingly to entail no more than membership in one of a number of identity groups that are popularly assumed to be analogically structured and comparably functioning, each with its own myth of Diaspora and its own rituals of solidarity.[11]

One European case that does bear some comparison with that of the United States is that of the Austro-Hungarian Empire. There, however, the Jews were generally felt to be the most different from the ethnic Germans; in the United States, by contrast, the presence of a large African American population has served to make Jews, as whites, more akin to the Anglo-Protestant majority. Nowhere—not in Germany, France, Italy, England, multi-ethnic Russia, or even the sprawling Habsburg domains—did a community of Jews do what happened in the United States and work out its relationship with a national society while symbolically paired with another "minority group" several times its demographic size yet many times weaker in economic power and uniquely central to the national history—the focal point, indeed, of a civil war. Whatever marginality might be attributed to Jews in the United States, even at the start of the twentieth century, to say nothing of what that marginality looked like at the start of the twenty-first century, it was not the same as the marginality experienced in most sites of the Diaspora.

Thus the peculiarity of the United States raises, even more than other cases, uncertainties about what significance should be assigned to Jewishness. It is not even always clear who should be counted as a Jew even for the purposes of analysis of the intellectual preeminence of Jews. Should we include persons who have a Jewish genetic inheritance but little Jewish cultural inheritance? Persons who prefer not to be counted? What does one do, for example, with the case of the political scientist Madeline Albright?

When Albright, as secretary of state, was confronted in 1997 with press reports that her parents had been Jewish, she found herself in the middle of an animated conversation about Jewish identity in the United States. Albright had grown up with no knowledge of her Jewish ancestry. Her parents, who fled Hitler's Europe and become Catholics, had concealed the truth. But now Albright herself, approaching sixty and living in a society where Jews were not persecuted, was free to be as Jewish as she might wish. To the disappointment of some, Albright appeared to be unchanged by the news of her Jewish ancestry. Indeed, she was so detached from this part of her past that she awkwardly denied the fact that she had learned of it privately some time before it became public. Hundreds of magazine and newspaper articles and editorials addressed what *The New Republic* called "Madeline Albright's Jewish problem."

Is Madeline Albright "really" Jewish? If so, in what sense? Can one be of "Jewish background," as Albright came to describe herself, but not be "Jewish"? Who decides, and on what basis? What is at stake, and for whom? The answers to these questions offered in the United States in our time are not likely to be the same as those that might be offered in Vichy France, or Imperial Germany, or contemporary Israel.

Consider also the case of the sociologist Robert K. Merton, who did not proclaim his Jewishness until 1994, half-a-century after he began to produce the magnificent series of papers that rendered him a giant of American sociology. In what sense is Merton Jewish? Is he Jewish for the purposes of an analysis of the preeminence of Jews in American science and scholarship, on the grounds of the assumption that as a child he must have absorbed some distinctly Jewish experiences? He would not have been counted, presumably, in the Carnegie study of 1969. And what if he had not declared himself in 1994? Would we then be justified in treating him as a Jew had we come to know the facts about his upbringing, on the methodological grounds that his very decision to change his name from Meyer H. Schkolnick to Robert K. Merton was probably rooted in an experience of anti-Jewish prejudice and of social marginality? Anyone can ascribe Jewish identity to

Merton by regarding him as a passive object, invoking one or more of the criteria by which he is a Jew. But are we to pay no attention to Merton's own definition of himself? Merton's case becomes more interesting when we reflect that, if he is counted, all three of the individuals who exercised the greatest influence on the historical, sociological, and philosophical study of science in the United States were born to Jewish parents yet lived their lives well outside of communal Jewry: Merton, Thomas S. Kuhn, and the Viennese Karl Popper.

The demographic overrepresentation of the liberated children of Jewish parents in the top leadership of the history, sociology, and philosophy of science can remind us of the kind of demographic information that keeps Veblen's question alive, just as the American circumstances I have reviewed can remind us of the uncertainty of the importance of the question. Perhaps the recent and contemporary United States is a society in which the old question of the intellectual preeminence of Jews in science and scholarship will somehow dissolve?

I doubt it. But whatever life the question leads in the future should be guided by the failures as well as the successes of the Veblen thesis. And surely the matter of Jewish preeminence in science and scholarship must be confronted in systematic relation to Jewish preeminence in other arenas of human endeavor, including those far removed from laboratories and campuses. Three of the four very top Bolsheviks, after all, were Kamenev, Trotsky, and Zinoviev—three Jews who stood with Lenin in 1917. Then there were Radek, Sokolnikov, Sverdlov, and Uritskii. We need a non-Red-baiting mode to confront the preeminence of Jews in Bolshevism, just as we need a non-anti-Semitic mode to confront the high percentage of billionaires who are Jews, and a non-ethnically chauvinistic mode to confront the overrepresentation of Jews among Nobel laureates. We need to find a way out of the booster-bigot trap, which quickly channels discussions of Jews in comparison to other groups into the booster's uncritical celebration of

Jewish achievements or the bigot's malevolent complaint about Jewish conspiracies. The whole issue of the role of Diaspora Jews in world history needs to be demystified. It needs to be treated, as Veblen himself in his best moments would have said, scientifically. It needs to be treated as a historical question like any other.

8

Rich, Powerful, and Smart

Jewish Overrepresentation Should Be Explained
Instead of Avoided or Mystified

*S*ome people think it unwise to speak at all of the demographic overrepre-
S sentation of Jews among the wealthiest, most politically powerful, and
most intellectually accomplished of Americans. I encounter this sentiment
among some readers made uncomfortable by my references to Jewish overrepresentation in my book of 1996, Science, Jews, and Secular Culture, *and*
in my article on the Veblen thesis, reprinted in this volume. Although I under-
stand the reasons for this reticence—e.g., do we want to feed anti-Semitic fan-
tasies of a Jewish conspiracy to run the world?—I believe the time has come
for historians and social scientists to apply their skills to the question. Anti-
Semitism is not so great a problem in the United States today to justify the
avoidance of the issue, and, as I argue in the intervention reprinted below, fail-
ure to address the question at this point in time may actually facilitate the per-
petuation of racist and other biocentric ideas. The truth is the best defense
against bigotry. The interlocking economic, political, and cultural conditions of
Diaspora Jewry over many centuries do much to explain Jewish preeminence
in the many practices of modernity, just as the conditions of slavery and Jim
Crow racism do much to explain the overrepresentation of black men in

American prisons. History, not essentialist ideas about communities of descent, tells us what we most need to know.

The immediate occasion for my writing this follow-up to my article on the Veblen thesis was an invitation from the editors of Jewish Quarterly Review *to contribute to a symposium on new directions in the study of American Jewish history. Shortly after I had drafted it I had the opportunity to read in manuscript the book of my colleague, Yuri Slezkine,* The Jewish Century *(Princeton, 2004). Slezkine's massively documented explanation for Jewish overrepresentation grounded in the specific historical conditions of the Jewish Diaspora in Europe strongly reinforced and extended my own thinking. I incorporated some of Slezkine's findings concerning the role of Jews in the Soviet bureaucracy. I want to take this occasion to again thank Slezkine for his contribution, a genuine breakthrough in the study of Jews, modernity and cosmopolitanism.*

This piece was first published in Jewish Quarterly Review *(Fall 2004): 596–602.*

In the closing scene of Philip Roth's *The Human Stain* (New York, 2000) two white men, one a Jew and one who might be called a "poor white," confront one another while standing on a sheet of white ice beneath which is an expanse of blackness. The dark water beneath the ice is an obvious symbol for a dead man the reader has learned was born black but had managed to pass as white, although at enormous personal cost. Indeed, his whiteness was like the ice, easily broken in the event of a change in the social weather. The Jew knows that the man born black had died some months earlier in the very waters of the now-ice-covered lake, murdered by the crude, uneducated man he was facing. But he can't prove it. After a few minutes of tense and evasive dialogue the Jew turns and walks away. The Jew, as a well-to-do, highly educated, self-aware person, is able to drive then to New Jersey to engage the black family of the dead man openly and honestly. But the local poor white, who never had much going for him to begin with and lost what humane capabilities he had when the government made him into a killing machine in Vietnam, remains on the white ice of the remote Berkshire lake. The "cracker" is imprisoned by his war-related clinical depression and by the petty prejudices against which his class and culture have given him all too little protection.

This scene, created by a writer whose unyielding preoccupation for more than thirty-five years has been the psychology of Jewishness in the historically specific conditions of late-twentieth-century America, displays features of American life that invite the sustained attention of historians: the success of Jews, and the relevance of a Jewish background to lives lived outside communal Jewry. Neither Roth nor his protagonist, Nathan Zuckerman, is significantly defined by the communal framework that is central to what we normally understand as "Jewish history." Yet their personae are deeply marked by a Jewish past. The Jewish experience that animates Roth's entire saga of class and culture, moreover, is not defined by the victimization that has been made all the more central to popular understandings of Jewish history by the Holocaust Museum near the National Mall in Washington, D.C. Rather, the salient Jewish experience is that of relative success, however refracted through neuroses and chaotic family dynamics.

Our national debates on public policy and our social science literature frequently discuss cases of underrepresentation in employment pools, in academia, in legislatures, in business leadership, and in the ranks generally of the middle class. But do not underrepresentation and overrepresentation form a logical syndrome? Should we not expect the same principles of causation to apply to both sides of the phenomenon? Might what we learn about the overrepresentation of particular descent groups help us to understand the underrepresentation of others, and vice versa? This might seem obvious, but the analysis of overrepresentation, and of the historical processes by which ethnoracial groups that were once underrepresented have become overrepresented, usually stops with the white color line. The Irish, the Italians, the Poles, and the Jews, we say, "became white." But invoking whiteness does not carry us very far. Rural poor whites are not overrepresented at Harvard and in the great brokerage firms. Philip Roth understands the difference very well.

By almost any index, Jews are demographically overrepresented among the wealthiest, the most politically powerful, and the most intellectually accomplished of Americans. Jewish experience since 1945 is the most dramatic single case in all of American history in which a stigmatized descent group that had been systematically discriminated against under the protection of law suddenly became overrepresented many times over in social spaces where its members' progress had been previously inhibited. Jews are not the only descent-defined group to prosper in the United States during the era since World War II, but Jewish success is such an inescapable fact that it invites emphasis and explanation, and in relation to explanations for the social destiny of other descent-defined groups. What explains the overrepresentation of Jews among the rich, the powerful, and the smart?

The failure to pursue this question implicitly fuels largely unexpressed speculations that Jews are, after all, superior—in the sense of being better equipped to cope with the challenges of a complex civilization—genetically to African Americans, Latinos, and American Indians, the groups whose underrepresentation is constantly at issue, and superior genetically also to non-Jewish whites. No sensitive person would say this, of course, for fear of giving offense. But the quiet suspicion that it may be true is an excellent reason to avoid the topic. I have encountered this sentiment, privately expressed by some scholars in the field, amid conversations about the overrepresentation of Jews among Nobel Prize winners and other leaders in scientific, scholarly, and artistic achievement. "I personally think it is genetic," one distinguished historian said to me, "but I would never say this in public."

Such presumptions feed the idea that too much talk about how quickly Jews rise to leadership positions in business, science, the arts, and in some political establishments might make other groups look bad. A sense of decency militates against this—why rub the collective noses of other groups in this reality?—and casts doubt on the wisdom and taste of colleagues who publish statistics on what percentage of billionaires, psychoanalysts, lawyers, left-leaning politicians, distinguished mathematicians, film directors, and chess champions are Jewish. Yet the grounds for this reticence diminish, if not disappear, if these statistics can be explained by taking full account of the conditions under which the various descent communities have been shaped. Avoiding the forthright historical and social-scientific study of the question perpetuates the mystification of Jewish history and subtly fuels the idea that the answer is really biological, and will serve to reinforce invidious distinctions between descent groups.

The Human Stain can be read as an inspiration to confront the ostensibly delicate question of Jewish overrepresentation with robust confidence in the tools of historians and social scientists. Hence I want to linger just a moment longer over what is probably Roth's most important novel. Roth gives us a black hero who lived his adult life as a highly successful white Jewish academic, but who in his own upbringing in a black community had been blessed with high degrees of social solidarity, cultural cohesion, literacy, and even commercial experience. The particular black family in which Coleman Silk was reared had all those things, and in abundance. Roth details exhaustively the circumstances of Silk's extended family, and the almost rabbinical-like learning of his father. If it was a light skin that enabled him to pass, it was a set of specific, sustaining conditions that equipped him to make such good use of his acquired whiteness, to perform so well as a classical scholar and as a dean. Roth does not attempt to develop a comprehensive comparative sociology of descent communities and of the terms on which color and color prejudice interact with class and culture, but *The Human Stain* does distinguish sharply between (a) an individual's membership in a descent community, and (b) an individual's coming into possession of the generic skills useful in modern society that have been unequally distributed by history among descent communities, even among those most victimized by European and European American prejudice. Roth urges us to see a black man through the social circumstances that are more common to Jews than to any other American descent community. Roth even endows a black character with the persona most precious to Roth: that of the obsessive, neurotic, Jewish intellectual. "Jewish like me," one might paraphrase John Howard Griffin on Roth/Zuckerman's behalf.

Being "Jewish" can mean, among other things, descent from many generations of people who experienced the conditions of the Jewish Diaspora in Europe. Among those conditions was the high rate of literacy sustained by rabbinic Judaism. But so, too, was the special economic position of Jews as an outsider group. They delivered a range of services about which the Christian and largely agricultural peoples dominant in Russia, the Hapsburg Monarchy, and many other states and empires were ambivalent.

The practice of trades and the handing of money, especially with interest, were essential to development of a modern, capitalist society and sufficiently in tension with traditional value systems to sharpen a division of labor. Jews often performed these vital services, while the non-Jewish majority could remain virtuous producers and honorable military men, and could hold themselves proudly aloof from moneylenders and middlemen. Boundary maintenance in this setting served the interests of both sides: if the outsider peoples mixed too much with the Poles or the Magyars or the Russians, the ability of the "outsiders" to do the "dirty work" diminished. Historians of European Jewry have explained all this to us many times. In order best to survive and prosper, Jews developed to a higher degree than other European descent groups the distinctive set of skills on which the modernization process most depended: calculation, language fluency, recordkeeping, close attention to detail, a facility for abstraction, and the mobility and flexibility required to move around and to deal with a variety of parties who often did not want much to do with each other. These are the very skills that form much of the basis for our modern notion of what it means to be "smart." The old wisecrack, usually offered affectionately, that Yiddish has at least nine words for "jerk" but only one for "tree" is emblematic of the people-centered as opposed to land-centered society and culture of the Central and Eastern European heartland of the Diaspora. The point I am making about the social conditions of many successive generations of Jewish experience in Europe is as simple as it is profound: those conditions endowed Jews with exactly the dispositions that turned out to be the most conducive to leadership in a host of distinctly modern callings in the North Atlantic West of the nineteenth and twentieth centuries.

Prominent among those callings was science, but so, too, was business. We do have an animated, long-term debate over what Thorstein Veblen, in a classic contribution to the debate, called "The Intellectual Preeminence of Jews in Modern Europe" (*Political Science Quarterly*, 1919). Jewish overrepresentation among Nobel Prize winners and on the faculties of leading universities is explained with reference to a variety of theories, many of them variations on Veblen's basic idea that the marginality of Jews to a Gentile-dominated society had generated a mentality of detachment and skepticism especially suited to the disinterested pursuit of learning. Veblen and most of his successors in this conversation have attended little to the comparable overrepresentation of Jews in high finance and on lists of the richest of the rich, perhaps because they do not want to retail stereotypes of Jewish bankers. Veblen, after all, was his generation's greatest scourge of a parasitic leisure class, but the plutocrats and genteel bandits of his most enduring prose in *The Theory of the Leisure Class* (New York, 1899) are never implied to be Jewish. As I have argued elsewhere (*Aleph* 2, 2002), Veblen's anti-commercial bias was so ferocious and his apotheosis of alienation so extravagant that he failed to consider the class position and economic function of Jews in contexts where it might have turned his explanation in a different direction. Inquiries into Jewish scientific and scholarly achievement often run on an independent track, seeking explanations that may or may not apply to other arenas in which Jews have distinguished themselves. But once the demographically disproportionate attainments of Jews in science and scholarship are placed alongside the statistically similar overrepresentation of Jews in the leadership of the professions and in business and finance, intellectual preeminence suddenly invites explanations that also account for these other instances of Jewish preeminence. The skills promoted by the conditions of the European Diaspora as summarized above surely help explain many kinds of Jewish success.

Those conditions also go far toward explaining another case of Jewish overrepresentation: among communists, during and after the Bolshevik Revolution, and in the international communist movement throughout Europe and North America. Three of the four very top Bolsheviks in the Revolution, after all, were Kamenev, Trotsky, and Zinoviev, three Jews who stood with Lenin in 1917. Lenin himself was later found to have a Jewish grandparent, although Stalin suppressed the information. Other Jews among the leading Bolsheviks included Radek, Sokolnikov, Sverdlov, and Uritskii. Yagoda, the head of the Soviet secret police under Stalin in the 1930s, was as much a child of the Diaspora as Einstein.

The skills that enabled Jews to take special advantage of the opportunities of a more industrialized, technologically oriented, specialist-intensive society in the United States and in Western and Central Europe also placed Jews at the forefront of the version of modernization undertaken by the Bolsheviks. Distinguished by a higher degree of literacy than any descent group in the Russian empire, including the ethnic Russians, the Jews who migrated to St. Petersburg and Moscow with the dissolution of the Pale of Settlement quickly established themselves in the professions even under the Tsarist regime, and, after the Revolution of 1917, in the state bureaucracy of the Soviet Union. But there was also a vital ideological component. A history of forced and invidious separation made many Jews enthusiastic about the idea of a universalist, socialist state, and Jews were heavily overrepresented among the makers of the Revolution and in the leadership of the new Soviet government. The dynamics of "enlightenment" within East European Jewry—the embracing of Western, secular learning and the storied revolts against the backwardness of the shtetl—interacted not only with the expansion of career opportunities within capitalist modernity, but with the explosion of career opportunities within a more radically modernizing movement and regime that promised to abolish the constraints that had kept Jews from realizing their humanity on the terms that non-Jews had been able to do. Although Stalin eventually turned the Soviet state in anti-Jewish directions, the earliest decades after the Revolution sustained the hope of Jews that communism was the swiftest and surest way to repudiate the tyranny of "blood and soil." How this course of events unfolded, and the extent of Jewish leadership of the Soviet bureaucracy, is clarified in the book by Yuri Slezkine, *The Jewish Century* (Princeton, N.J., 2004).

Fully incorporating the study of the Russian-Soviet case into the discussion of the question of Jewish overrepresentation in elites is wise for three closely related reasons. First, it promises to display the power of historical and social-scientific explanations to neutralize prejudicial, mystified, and ethnoracially essentialist ideas about Jews and their role in modern societies. The more we understand how the conditions of the Jewish Diaspora in Europe fostered Jewish participation in the Russian Revolution and the Soviet state, the less credible become suspicions that this participation was caused by something else, such as a peculiarly Jewish will to power. Second, the actual explaining of Jewish overrepresentation among the Bolsheviks, and among their political allies in the United States and other Western countries, promises greater emancipation from the notorious "booster-bigot trap" according to which the prominence of Jews in one arena or another is reduced to ethnic chauvinism on the one hand or malevolent complaints about Jewish conspiracies on the other. The "good" conversation about Jewish Nobel Prize winners (something to be proud of) and the "bad" conversation about Jewish communists (something the mere mention of which plays into the hands of anti-Semites) can be increasingly replaced by a conversation that recognizes the historically contingent character of all episodes of Jewish overrepresentation. Third, the Russian-Soviet case is a dramatic reminder that some very important history has been made by men and women who (a) were deeply marked by the conditions of the Jewish Diaspora in Europe, but (b) did not identify themselves as Jews. The same point can be made about some men and women in the United States and the countries of Western Europe—there were many who distinguished themselves in one context or another without affirming any affiliation with a Jewish community—but the Russian-Soviet case is enormous and centers on people who actually rejected Jewish identity and invested themselves in the building of a society where Jewishness would be a category with little meaning.

This last point can underscore for us an important issue concerning the scope of the field to which this *Jewish Quarterly Review* issue is addressed, and the location of its borders with adjacent, collegial fields. The role in history played by people who were shaped by the conditions of the Jewish Diaspora is a much broader site for inquiry than the history of communal Jewry. Yet most of what gets classified as "Jewish history" or "Jewish studies," I hope it is fair to observe, is focused on people who identified themselves as Jews or whose destiny was greatly affected by their being classified as Jews by someone else. Perhaps that is as it should be, or perhaps the borders need to be altered. But scholars have good reason to confront the challenge of dealing with historical actors who were obviously shaped by the conditions of the Jewish Diaspora in Europe yet affiliated only nominally or not at all with any Jewish community and/or were only rarely treated by Gentiles in any special way on account of their Jewish ancestry. The secular men and women of Jewish background who did so much to advance the revolutionary movement in the Russian empire and to staff the Soviet regime in its early decades are perhaps the most vivid examples of this syndrome, but the syndrome applies, also, to many scientists and financiers in the North Atlantic West, and to many of the men and women who led in the development of psychoanalysis, Hollywood, modernist movements in the arts, and other endeavors that have not been defined ethnoreligiously. If such people are not Jewish enough for their projects and their accomplishments, nefarious or noble, to be included in the mainstream of Jewish history and Jewish studies as focused on communal Jewry, surely there is still something Jewish here to be studied. We all know that Mordecai Kaplan, Abraham Cahan, Stephen Wise, and Irving Howe were figures in American Jewish history, but what about J. Robert Oppenheimer, Robert K. Merton, Thomas S. Kuhn, Walter Lippmann, Julius Rosenberg, Joyce Brothers, Benny Goodman, Ayn Rand, and Madeline Albright?

To be sure, there is a danger of overdetermination: one can try to explain too much with reference to a Jewish background. But that is where statistics are helpful: when descendants of a Diaspora are found to be overrepresented, the greater the overrepresentation the more we should consider explanations grounded in the conditions of the Diaspora. The overrepresentation of Asian Americans in certain sectors is now being analyzed with reference to the distinctive pre-immigration history and immigration patterns of Americans of Japanese, Chinese, Vietnamese, Bengali, Punjabi, etc., descent. It makes methodological sense to explain cases of overrepresentation with the same analytic tools we use to explain underrepresentation. If the overrepresentation of African American males in prisons can be explained, as it often is by our historians and social scientists, with reference to slavery, Jim Crow, and the larger history of the institutionalized debasement of black people, so, too, can the overrepresentation of Jews in other social spaces be explained by the same principles and methods. Philip Roth, in creating the life of the "black" Coleman Silk in dialectical relation to the experience of Jews and poor whites, understands this as well as we historians do.

9

Cultural Relativism

*A*nthropologists were the grand exemplars of cosmopolitanism in the United States during the twentieth century. Sympathetically engaged with cultures around the world, the anthropologists relentlessly reminded their American readers that their own practices and tastes, however cherished and however resoundingly affirmed as God-given norms, were scarcely more than bubbles on an ocean of human behavior. This radically deprovincializing impulse gradually came to be known by the name of "cultural relativism," the character and history of which I was asked to clarify by the editors of the Cambridge History of Science.

Since the term had become highly contested, my task was partly to explain how and why so many people were angered by one another's assertions as to the true meaning of cultural relativism. Hence this intellectual history of the cultural relativist movement within and beyond the professional community of anthropologists distinguishes between the scientific-methodological and the critical-ideological dimensions of the work of Franz Boas and his followers, and argues that the reluctance of many of the anthropologists themselves to appreciate this distinction has led to many of the quarrels that extend to our own time. I also try to explain how a series of world-historical changes in the decades after Margaret Mead and Ruth Benedict popularized cultural relativism have altered the questions that western intellectuals bring to the scrutiny of the world's diverse cultures, rendering the formulations of the classic cultural relativists at once anachronistic and banal. Along the way, I point to the role played in this story by Jewish intellectuals, more prominent in the leadership of cultural anthropologists than in that of any social science discipline in the United States of the relevant era.

This article first appeared in Theodore M. Porter and Dorothy Ross, eds., The Cambridge History of Science, VII: The Modern Social Sciences *(New York: Cambridge University Press, 2003), 708–20.*

Of prominent concepts that owe their credibility and popularity to social science, "cultural relativism" is unusual for having received so little clarification from social scientists. The concept is properly associated with a group of anthropologists who flourished in the United States during the second quarter of the twentieth century and who argued, first, that culture rather than biology explained the range of human behavior, and, second, that the sheer diversity of this behavior as seen throughout the world should inspire respect and tolerance rather than invidious judgments. But these anthropologists tried only episodically to fix the meaning of "cultural relativism," and their successors have proven impatient with the terms on which it has been implicated in later debates over moral philosophy, human rights, multiculturalism, and postmodernism. A phrase that became familiar as an affirmation of liberal values and cosmopolitan tolerance came to be associated instead with the defense of parochial cultures that sanction the abuse of women, and with the dismissal of the ideal of a common humanity. References to "cultural relativism" were more abundant in the 1980s and 1990s than ever before, but the meaning of the term and its relation to the anthropological movement said to be responsible for it were more elusive than ever. Hence "cultural relativism" is a topic without an agreed-upon referent. Indeed, the debate over just what cultural relativism is constitutes a vital part of its history.

The central claim of cultural relativism, according to Melville J. Herskovits (1895–1963), the anthropologist who embraced the term the most persistently and with the least ambivalence, is that *"Judgments are based on experience, and experience is interpreted by each individual in terms of his own enculturation."*[1] This emphatic statement of 1955 may imply that questions of right and wrong, and of truth and falsity demand different answers depending on one's particular culture. But neither Herskovits nor the other anthropologists of his cohort were eager to put it so starkly. Indeed, crisp definitions of cultural relativism—that it means "truth and goodness are relative to your culture," or "one culture is as good as another"— have been the staple of its critics, who have found themselves ridiculed, in turn, for failing to understand it.

"There is not one of its critics in a hundred" who has got "right" what cultural relativism originally was, Clifford Geertz exploded in 1984, while complaining that critics had reduced it to "regarding Hitler as just a fellow with unstandard tastes." Geertz, whose views gain significance from his standing as one of the world's most accomplished anthropologists, was more incisive in explaining what cultural relativism was not than in declaring its positive essence. Getting cultural relativism right, according to Geertz, was not a matter of sharpening the formulations of philosophical doctrine, or of providing dictionary writers with a sounder list of synonyms. Rather, it was a matter of recognizing one "way of thinking" in relation to the rival ways of thinking against which this one had been developed in the late nineteenth and early twentieth centuries.[2]

This resolutely historical approach to the meaning of "cultural relativism" has much to recommend it. The anthropological exploration of cultural diversity, especially among distant peoples, unsettled inherited assumptions about the North Atlantic West. Were the moral codes produced by European civilization really the best ones, worthy of being foisted upon the rest of the globe? Anthropologists were the Westerners who looked the longest and hardest at the "Zunis and Dohomeys," Geertz observed, and who came to grips the most honestly with the sheer diversity of the arrangements by which people manage somehow to live, and even to flourish. No wonder it was these explorers of alterity who were the most inclined to insist that "rushing to judgment" about the practices of foreign peoples "is more than a mistake, it's a crime."[3]

This attitude of reserved judgment toward the prodigious expanse of human life is the core of the "relativistic" way of thinking that Geertz urged us to thank for discovering "that the world does not divide into the pious and the superstitious; that there are sculptures in jungles and paintings in deserts; that political order is possible without centralized power and principled justice without codified rules; that the norms of reason were not fixed in Greece, the evolution of morality not consummated in England."

Another contribution made by these ethnographic pioneers, Geertz added, was their insistence that "we see the lives of others through lenses of our own grinding and that they look back on ours through ones of their own." To this string of hard-won, cosmopolitan insights Geertz contrasted not only the old ethnocentric, parochial confidence that one's own tribe was a model for the species, but also an ancient faith that often fosters arrogance: the faith that we can locate morality "beyond culture" and that we can attain knowledge that is unmediated by the morality and culture of the knower. This extreme anti-relativist faith animates critics of cultural relativism, according to Geertz, just as the rejection of this faith is what most defines it.[4]

The active center of the historic movement in twentieth-century social science that goes by the name of cultural relativism was *a principled doubt that "our" people are right while groups who do things differently are wrong.* But behind the debate over the meaning of the term flagging the movement, and behind Geertz's own intervention in this debate, is an uneasy relationship between two applications of this principled doubt. One application is methodological. The other is ideological. Only by recognizing both, and by appreciating the dynamic interaction of the two, can we achieve a history of cultural relativism that avoids the mistakes against which Geertz warns, and that explains the quarrel over its meaning.

Methodologically, cultural relativism has been a *social scientific* device designed to enable anthropologists to confront, and to attain reliable knowledge about, aspects of *foreign* cultures they might not grasp adequately were they caught up always in judging how the people they study measure up to the standards of the inquirer's home culture. It is this method that Geertz praises for having liberated us from a number of provincial conceits, and that he strives to separate from the dubious, sweeping philosophical claims attributed to cultural relativism by its detractors. But cultural relativism has been more than a scholarly will to see someone else's culture from the inside. The second, ideological use of moral and epistemic humility has brought cultural relativism directly into philosophy and "culture wars."

Ideologically, cultural relativism has been a *critical* device fashioned for the purpose of undermining the authority of aspects of a *home* culture. The climax of Margaret Mead's (1901–1978) significantly subtitled *Coming of Age in Samoa: A Psychological Study of Primitive Youth for Western Civilization* (1928) was a breezy, homiletic commentary on the customs of the United States and Samoa, suggesting that middle class Americans of the 1920s might improve the rearing of their adolescent girls by taking some cues from the sexually relaxed life of the South Pacific.[5] Reflection on the possible implications for "Western Civilization" of what had been discovered about other cultures, especially "primitive" ones, is what made anthropology in the cultural relativist mode a major episode in the intellectual history of the twentieth century, rather than simply another movement within a discipline.

The scientific virtues of cultural relativism were advanced the most vocally, and with the most public notice, by men and women who invited attention as social critics, not simply as practitioners of an esoteric *Wissenschaft*. Some of the relativizing anthropologists went on to offer cultural relativism as a "philosophy." Herskovits did this frequently, including in his widely used college textbook of 1948, *Man and His Works*, inviting rebuttals of exactly the kind that struck Geertz, a generation later, as misunderstandings of the epistemic and moral humility that anthropologists had contributed.[6] When cultural relativism's detractors address it as a perspective on value-disputes within the North Atlantic West, and evaluate it in its capacity as a theory of truth and value, they do so in an atmosphere created by some of Geertz's predecessors.

Franz Boas and the Reaction against Evolutionary Anthropology

Cultural relativism has its immediate origins in an argument within the ranks of scholars who faced the enormous panorama of human diversity in the late nineteenth and very early twentieth centuries. Most of the pioneers in the scientific study of human diversity were "evolutionists" who envisioned a gradual, progressive development of the human species. E. B. Tylor in England and Lewis Henry Morgan in the United States were among the most creative of these early anthropologists, who looked upon the "primitive" peoples of their contemporary world as living at an earlier stage of an evolutionary process that culminated in the "civilized" societies of the North Atlantic West. Even scholars who took a relatively generous view of the varieties of humankind and found the scope of human life humbling adopted this hierarchical perspective, which served in many cases to diminish the threat to assumptions of Western superiority that was potentially posed by the discovery of more and more peoples in the Amazon basin, Africa, and elsewhere. The mere presence in the contemporary world of large numbers of such people proved how small a percentage of the human species had ever lived according to the rules and tastes prevailing in modern Europe. The notion of social evolution enabled Westerners to categorize each new discovery of a past or present society as occupying a certain stage in the general progress of humanity. As Thomas Trautmann has explained, these nineteenth-century thinkers in effect laid "the great chain of being" on its side, so that the traditional hierarchies supported by this ancient construct—according to which life forms were distributed from lower to higher on an ascending, vertical scale—were rendered temporal, taking the form of a horizontal timeline.[7] This hierarchical, evolutionary analysis of human diversity was subject to great variations, ranging, on the eve of the revolt against it, from the conservatism displayed in William Graham Sumner's *Folkways* (1906) to the savage attack on progress-retarding elites in Thorstein Veblen's *Theory of the Leisure Class* (1899).

The normative assumptions of the evolutionists were not challenged systematically and effectively until Franz Boas (1858–1942) published *The Mind of Primitive Man* in 1911. This book, which consolidated and elaborated upon arguments Boas had been developing for more than two decades in scientific journals, held that the gap between "primitive" and "civilized" peoples was not nearly so great as had been supposed, and that patterns in human behavior should be understood less in terms of progressive stages than in terms of coexisting, autonomous, distinctive cultures. Boas's critique of evolutionary anthropology was directed especially against its emphasis on biology and race, as opposed to culture, but as Boas explained the workings of culture he stressed the capacity of cultural conditioning to establish standards for conduct and rationality. The minds of primitive peoples might seem irrational from the perspective of the North Atlantic West in 1911, but those minds, including those of the Indians in the Pacific Northwest studied by Boas, worked according to rationality of their own. The "general effect of Boas's argument," George W. Stocking, Jr., has observed, "was to show that the behavior" of all humans, "regardless of race or cultural stage, was determined by a traditional body of habitual behavior patterns" passed on from generation to generation. Once "the multiplicity of *cultures* took the place of the cultural *stages* of savagery, barbarism, and civilization," Stocking continues, the varieties of culture "were no more easily brought within one standard of evaluation than they were within one system of explanation."[8] Boas's emphasis on the integrity and autonomy of each culture's value-system had much in common with the rudimentary philosophical anthropology sketched a century before by the German theorist, Johann Gottfried von Herder.

Yet Boas stopped well short of the inference that no standards could be defended over others. Stocking points out that Boas matched his advocacy of tolerance and respect for cultural difference, on the one hand, with a hope, on the other, that more defensible standards for human conduct could be developed if one took into account the experience of cultures beyond the one in which he and his fellow Westerners had grown up. Even in the context of Boas's "relativistic, pluralistic critique of evolutionism," Stocking cautions, "Boas still found in the general development of human culture at least qualified affirmation of the specific values most central to his personal world view: reason, freedom, and human fellowship."[9]

Boas understood that these values were not fully institutionalized in the society in which he lived. He argued against the racist characterizations of Jews, Asians, Slavs, and other groups put forth by advocates of immigration restriction. Boas was the only American scientist of stature to try to expose the scientific inadequacy of many of these racist assertions prior to the mid-1920s. Yet even had Boas been less active than he was in trying to reduce racism in public life, his scientific work was certainly directed against aspects of his home culture of which he was critical. To suggest that among Boas's motives was a desire to counteract racism and invidious hierarchies is not to diminish his achievements as a scientist, but only to recognize the ideological as well as the methodological functions of Boas's work.

The ideological as well as the methodological appeal of a relativistic approach to the study of human diversity was visible in the disciples Boas won through his published work and through his teaching of students at Columbia University in New York City from the turn of the century through the 1920s. Columbia was then an important setting for the interaction of Anglo-Protestant students and faculty with intellectuals of Jewish origin from both Eastern Europe and Germany. In this milieu, commentators on the American scene developed a non-invidious, respectful attitude toward immigrant groups that paralleled the outlook toward foreign peoples espoused by Boas and his students. No promoter of this cosmopolitan perspective on the United States was more eloquent, nor in the long run more warmly remembered, than Randolph Bourne, who was inspired by Boas's lectures at Columbia and who reviewed *The Mind of Primitive Man* appreciatively.[10] Many who admired Boas were either of immigrant Jewish stock, like Boas himself, who had come from Germany at the age of twenty-nine, or were, like Bourne and Mead, Anglo-Protestants reacting against what they perceived as the narrowness of their ancestral culture.

Boas's students and protégés included, in addition to Mead and Herskovits, Ruth Benedict (1887–1948), Alexander Goldenweiser (1883–1953), Alfred Kroeber (1876–1960), Robert Lowie (1883–1957), Elsie Clews Parsons (1875–1941), Paul Radin (1883–1959), Edward Sapir (1884–1939), and Leslie Speir (1893–1961). Of this group of ten leading anthropologists, half were Jewish, four had been born in Europe, and three were women. The leadership of no other social scientific or humanistic discipline of that generation in the United States displayed this demographic mix. American-born Anglo-Protestant males were dominant in the academic profession, but few became anthropologists in the Boasian mode. The early constituency of cultural relativism thus lends credibility to the common speculation that marginality is conducive to the development of relativistic perspectives on culture.

Boas's Students and the Development of Cultural Relativism

Are We Civilized? The title of Lowie's book of 1929 was well chosen. The point of reference is "we," and the question to be asked is whether the distinction between the civilized and the uncivilized stands up to the scrutiny of anthropologists. Here in full flower is the principled doubt that our ways are the culmination of the progressive development of the species. And here at its most confident is the classic technique of juxtaposing the norms of readers to the norms operative elsewhere. "If you saw a man spitting at another, you would infer that he was expressing contempt," Lowie began this book, but "in East Africa among the Jagga Negroes" spitting "is a kind of blessing." There is nothing "natural," Lowie explained, in our conventional wisdom that spitting is done "in order to show loathing." Folks who spit to show goodwill are not any less civilized, anthropology tells us, than folks who spit to show the opposite. But Lowie's relativistic perspective did not preclude judgments, or a sense of progress. He favored a tolerant cosmopolitanism and a "united humanity" that struggled against the endless sequence of sectarian, parochial enclosures erected by his fellows.[11]

Lowie's *Are We Civilized?* represented the cultural relativist movement at its most glib. Mead was more earnest, not only in *Coming of Age In Samoa*, but in *Growing Up in New Guinea: A Study in Comparative Education* (1930) and her thirty-two additional books. Lowie, Mead, Herskovits and the other Boasians made substantial, specific ethnographic contributions that have a place in the history of science quite apart from the cultural relativism that helped propel their ethnographies and that, in turn, provided the raw materials for its articulation. But it was primarily in their capacity as public intellectuals that Boas's students developed cultural relativism. The Boasian anthropologists of the 1920s, 1930s, and 1940s, Richard Handler has summarized, "took seriously the duty of the scholar and scientist to make specialized knowledge accessible to the citizens of a modern society."[12]

It was therefore fitting that the single book that did the most to define cultural relativism in the minds of the public, and of anthropologists, was written by a theorist and gifted writer who did no field work. Benedict's legendary book of 1934, *Patterns of Culture*, explicitly espoused "cultural relativity" as a theoretical doctrine. It was recognized, at the end of the twentieth century, as one of the most widely read books ever produced by a social scientist in any discipline. It is the central document in the history of cultural relativism.

The core chapters of *Patterns of Culture* offered descriptions of Dobu, Kwakiutl, and Zuni ways of life. The variations in customs, from one society to another, illustrated how differently the peoples of the world had selected traits from what Benedict described idealistically as the "great arc of culture." Each selection from this virtually infinite inventory of human possibilities went into the creating of a distinctive culture, best understood as analogous to the personality of an individual. Each culture was thus a coherent whole, a system that worked within its own terms, deserving, of course, the respect that honorable people give to their individual neighbors. In trying to convey the integrity and dignity of the various cultures of the world, Benedict invoked a powerful, romantic image that became an icon for cultural relativism's benign vision of human difference: she quoted an aged California Indian as saying that God, "in the beginning," had provided every people with "a cup of clay, and from this cup they drank their life." Speaking of his own people, the Indian added, "our cup is broken now."[13] Here, as often in the pages of *Patterns of Culture*, it was Benedict's literary skills, not the scientific findings of her field-working colleagues, that most advanced the cause of cultural relativism.

That cause was, for Benedict, indissolubly bound-up with a desire for the reform of Benedict's home culture through the reduction of intolerance, prejudice, violence, and greed. If Benedict projected a non-judgmental attitude in general, her descriptions of the Dobu, the Kwakiutl, and the Zuni were subtly moralistic, and were interspersed with rueful observations about the culture of her readers. Benedict emphasized the cruelty that was routine among the Dobu of New Guinea, and concluded her account by noting that other societies had largely eliminated the "extreme forms of animosity and malignancy" still seen among the Dobu. As Stocking has observed, Benedict presented foreign cultures almost as "pathological parodies of the worst aspects of the puritan and robber-baron traditions" of her own society. The point of learning about cultural diversity was eventually one of judgment at home: "We may train ourselves," wrote Benedict, "to pass judgment upon the dominant traits of our own civilization," among which she counted "capitalism" and "war." Benedict did not specify the criteria by which "we can evaluate objectively" these and other traits of our "Western civilization," but the chief point of reference throughout *Patterns of Culture* was her own society. She explicitly prescribed John Dewey's conception of "social engineering" guided by "rationally selected goals" that could be chosen once the full range of possibilities for human life were gleaned from the results of anthropological study.[14] Benedict's plea for tolerance resonated well with readers who saw a globe filled with examples of intolerance—Nazism, Imperialism, Stalinism, Racism—that were offensive to liberal ideas of freedom and human dignity. Benedict pitted liberal hope against a world of challenging ethnocentrisms and repressions. Although Benedict did not eschew judgments, what *Patterns of Culture* conveyed the most compellingly was a sense that negative judgments about human conduct were very likely to be wrong.

What perspective should one take toward cultures that were, themselves, intolerant? Did not the logic of cultural relativism require that "we" respect other cultures that work on the basis of values antithetical to the liberal cosmopolitanism espoused in *Patterns of Culture?* Benedict and her allies did not find this concern nearly as pressing as did discussants of cultural relativism during the 1980s and 1990s. By then, a host of intellectual and political transformations within and beyond the North Atlantic West—to which this article attends below—had given urgency to questions that had struck Benedict, Herskovits, and their associates as nit-picking distractions from the big issues. But to the "small" issues the classical cultural relativists did respond occasionally, as when Herskovits, in a 1942 call to arms against the Axis Powers, suggested tentatively that "the concept of freedom should be realistically redefined as the right to be exploited in terms of the patterns of one's own culture."[15]

Herskovits offered this provocative thought as an aside. He alluded to the damage done to African autonomy by well-meaning European efforts to end "slavery" and "human sacrifice," but the ease with which Herskovits inserted this comment within a justification for warfare against the Nazis revealed the depth of two of assumptions found frequently in the writings of cultural relativists. First, boundaries between cultures were sharp and clear. Second, the apparent evils internal to a given culture could be distinguished from the bona fide evil of an assault by agents of one culture on another culture. Herskovits had no doubt that his culture was being assaulted, but in urging its defense he was extremely cautious. In a formulation implying that some anti-Axis Westerners influenced by cultural relativism might indeed wonder if their own culture had a warrant deep enough to justify warfare, Herskovits said that we must "clearly understand that it is possible to reaffirm in positive terms the fundamental tenets by which we live."[16] But was Germany, one might ask, part of "our" culture, enabling us to take issue with practices internal to Germany even had the Germans kept within their own internationally recognized borders? Or was Germany a different culture, deserving of the same liberty to abuse its own that Herskovits asked for Africans?

This question is not one the classical cultural relativists were eager to explore. Their own culture was sometimes as large as "the West" and at other times constricted enough to exclude the Nazis. Herskovits often complained of the tendency of discussants to harp on the Nazi case, which he seemed to regard as a wedge that threatened to divide cultural relativists who could agree except on the most extreme and difficult of cases. "Most frequently," Herskovits noted wearily in 1956, the question is asked, "granting the validity of each people's way of life, and the respect to be accorded these ways by peoples whose values are different, what should we do in the face, let us say, of the Nazi policy of the extermination of the German Jews?" Such questions are "not easy to answer," he said, but he went on quickly to make two points. First, "a philosophy based on the scientific findings of cross-cultural study does not imply unilateral tolerance of ideas other than one's own," and, second, "cultural relativism in and of itself does not provide all the rules or all the answers for living in a modern world."[17]

Herskovits's colleague Lowie approached the Nazi question more directly in "Empathy, or 'Seeing from Within,'" an essay that Herskovits admired for what he called its "tough-mindedness." Lowie, writing shortly before his death in 1957, declared that "Nazism furnishes a capital test of ethnological maturity." This admirable quality, Lowie explained, is to avoid passing "moral judgment" on the basis of standards alien to a given culture. He credited Herder with the sound insight that "every people and every epoch must be judged in accordance with local and temporal conditions, not by any extraneous standards." But Lowie's exemplification of this "ethnological maturity" turned out not to display "empathy" toward the super-aliens who carried out atrocities. There were "good and bad Germans," explained Lowie, who gave numerous examples of the good. "Aryan friends helped Mrs. Rosenfeld to escape across the Swiss border, at the risk of their own lives," Lowie said of one of many cases he cited to show how mistaken it was to think of all Germans as cruel and anti-Semitic. "It is absurd to suppose that any considerable number" of Germans "approved the pogroms of 1938 and later," he added. What appeared to be an ethnography of Nazism, enabling his readers to understand the behavior patterns of a truly foreign culture "as the native sees them," quickly became, instead, an argument that the culture of the Germans in the 1930s and 1940s was highly variable, and sustained many "good" Germans who behaved as his readers would like to think of themselves as behaving had they been Germans during the Third Reich.[18]

Lowie and Herskovits had difficulty taking seriously the possibility there could be too much tolerance. Yet this possibility gained credibility as the campaign for tolerance achieved a large measure of success, and as many prominent features of the world confronted by the classical cultural relativists were transformed.

The Uncertain Legacy of Cultural Relativism

Four major transformations affected the setting in which cultural relativism was discussed in the later decades of the twentieth century. The first, which altered the power relationships within which culture was embedded, was geopolitical. The European colonial empires were replaced by dozens of new nation-states during the two decades immediately following World War II. Many of the peoples studied by anthropologists were located in parts of Africa and Asia where political authority was transferred from the French, British, and Dutch to a variety of indigenous and creole elites. The new governments, while close enough in culture to the "natives" of anthropological lore to bring upon themselves some of the legitimacy conferred by a cultural relativist perspective, usually inherited political borders drawn by the old colonial powers. As a result, the new states embraced several different peoples. Where did one culture end and another begin, and how did these cultures come to be constituted, in part, by their modes of interacting with a civic authority that was ostensibly "theirs" yet in many cases was the tool of an alien ethnic group? These complications were later compounded by the consolidation of a world-capitalist economy managed by multinational corporations and serviced by an international labor force on multiple sites of production: this economy simultaneously universalized and particularized the culture it touched. The mechanisms of commercial exchange and the technology of rapid communications promoted the use of the English language and the dissemination of American popular culture throughout the world, while the targeting of particular markets for certain consumer goods reinforced some traditional cultural patterns. In the meantime, in reaction against the capacity of the global economy to spread the culture of the North Atlantic West, many groups, especially in heavily Muslim countries, promoted "intolerant" varieties of religious and ethnic particularism that were articulated in open conflict with Western cosmopolitanism. Cultures became harder to see as cups of clay inherited from time immemorial.

The second transformation entailed a shift in the winds of doctrine within the academic and literary elites of the North Atlantic West. From the 1960s onward, the arrogance and invidiousness against which the cultural relativists had fought was placed more sharply on the defensive by a host of thinkers who emphasized the "situated" character of scientific and ethical judgments. The first and by far the most influential of these new "relativistic" works was Thomas S. Kuhn's (1922–1996) *The Structure of Scientific Revolutions* (1962). Kuhn argued that even the most warranted of truth-claims in the most developed of the sciences depended on the workings of contingent, historically specific human communities. Although Kuhn did not adopt the label, "relativist," he was routinely called one and his work stimulated an enormous controversy over "cognitive relativism." The self-styled "Kuhnian" Richard Rorty, in *Philosophy and the Mirror of Nature* (1979), went farther in the direction of denying the role of non-discursive constraints on knowledge, and in later writings defended ethnocentrism as a basis for cognitive progress and political commonwealth. Geertz's two most widely appreciated books, *The Interpretation of Cultures*

(1973) and especially *Local Knowledge* (1984), contributed substantially to the mood of epistemic and moral humility. Hence the intelligentsia underwent a transition "from species to ethnos," in which an earlier generation's struggle to overcome parochialism in the interest of a more truly universal perspective was replaced by a new generation's doubts that any universalist perspective could be anything more than a false front for this or that ethnos-specific frame of reference. Although these thinkers of the later decades of the twentieth century rarely invoked "cultural relativism," the continuity between the new relativism and the old was sufficient to win an audience for commentators who lumped them together, and even for some who appropriated the term for contemporary polemics without attending at all to the classical cultural relativists. Under the sign of "cultural relativism," the British philosopher Christopher Norris in 1996 wrote a vigorous critique of Kuhn, Rorty, Walzer, and Geertz—as well as of Ludwig Wittgenstein, and of Michel Foucault, Jacques Derrida, François Lyotard, and a number of other recent French theorists—without even mentioning any of the Boasian anthropologists.[19] "Cultural relativism" had entered a phase of its history altogether detached from its origins, from its early development, and even from its most popular expressions.

The third transformation was the development within the United States of the movement that came eventually to be called "multiculturalism," which called into question the monolithic, integrated, and bounded character of the "home" culture. Multiculturalism began in the late 1960s and early 1970s as an effort to recognize and appreciate the cultural diversity of a national community that had been represented more holistically than could be sustained by the empirical work of social scientists and humanists. The notion of a single "American culture" was also politically suspect in an era when a variety of ethnoracial groups, especially African Americans, were protesting the virtual erasure, by Anglo-Protestants, of their contributions to the cultural life of the United

States. From the late 1970s onward, multiculturalism was increasingly defined by an alliance with affirmative action programs for non-whites, resulting in greater emphasis on the cultures associated with African Americans, Asian Americans, Latinos, and Native Americans in distinction from European Americans. Although "culture" was omnipresent in each of these demographic blocs, the blocs were identified less by cultural patterns than by skin color: black, yellow, brown, red, and white. Hence a movement that was broadly cultural relativist in orientation developed in ways that cut deeply against the Boasian emphasis on culture as distinct from genetically transferred physical characteristics.

The fourth transformation was the growth of an international feminist movement that challenged the ethical autonomy of particular cultures with a new version of human rights universalism. Although the genital cutting of young females in Muslim-controlled states was the most widely discussed example of a practice that created tension between the rights of women and the rights of cultures, during the 1980s and 1990s feminists identified a wide range of practices in many parts of the world that invited external pressure for reform. The devaluation of female babies in China was another example. Within the United States, feminists criticized the "cultural defense" against criminal prosecution in cases of wife-beating and child abuse. Eager to distance themselves from imperialist and missionary interventions in indigenous cultures, these feminists usually tried to work as closely as possible with groups of women within the societies where human rights violations were believed to be taking place. It was in relation to the human rights of females that the term "cultural relativism" was the most often mentioned in the 1980s and 1990s.

These four major transformations have rendered less defensible several of the ideas advanced by the classical cultural relativists. It is increasingly difficult to locate and maintain the clear boundaries around which the original cultural relativist program was organized. The conversation about cultural difference is too well developed to allow one to make philosophical claims and then refuse to support them with arguments. Social scientists and other intellectuals who struggle against intolerance and ethnocentrism now require tools sharper than those bequeathed by the classical cultural relativists. Yet at the end of the twentieth century, the principled doubt that "our" people are right while groups who do things differently are wrong is more widely and deeply entrenched in the intelligentsia of the North Atlantic West than ever before in recorded history. If this fact renders obsolete the emphases and tone of the classical cultural relativists, it also marks the extent of their victory.

Notes

Index

Notes

Chapter 1. Amalgamation and Hypodescent

1. Peggy Pascoe, "Miscegenation Law, Court Cases, and Ideologies of 'Race' in Twentieth-Century America," *Journal of American History* 83 (June 1996): 64–65; Robert A. Pratt, "Crossing the Color Line: A Historical Assessment and Personal Narrative of *Loving v. Virginia*," *Howard Law Journal* 41 (1998), as rpt. in Kevin R. Johnson, ed., *Mixed Race America and the Law* (New York: New York University Press, 2003), 56–59.

2. Hannah Arendt, "Reflections on Little Rock," *Dissent* (Winter 1959): 79. This incident is analyzed by Werner Sollors, "Of Mules and Mares in a Land of Difference; or, Quadrupeds All?" *American Quarterly* 42 (June 1990), esp. 173–77.

3. Sidney Hook, *New Leader*, April 13, 1959.

4. An important example of open opposition to miscegenation laws during the 1960s was William D. Zabel, "Interracial Marriage and the Law," *Atlantic* (October 1965): 75–79.

5. *Loving v. Commonwealth of Virginia*, 388 U.S. 1; 87 S. Ct. 1817; 1967 U.S. Maryland repealed its miscegenation statute just prior to the court's action. Fourteen states in the Far West and upper Middle West repealed their statutes between 1952 and 1966.

6. Polling data are reviewed in one of the most carefully detailed monographs yet addressed to the history of ethnoracial mixture in the United States, Paul Spickard, *Mixed Blood: Intermarriage and Ethnic Identity in Twentieth-Century America* (Madison: University of Wisconsin Press, 1989), esp. 192–93.

7. Martin Kilmjin, "Trends in Black/White Intermarriage," *Social Forces* 72 (1993): 119–46.

8. A. Leon Higgenbotham and Barbara K. Kopytoff, "Racial Purity and Interracial Sex in the Law of Colonial and Antebellum Virginia,"

in Werner Sollors, ed., *Interracialism: Black-White Intermarriage in American History, Literature, and Law* (New York: Oxford University Press, 2000), 138–39. Higgenbotham and Kopytoff quote the South African minister of the interior's presentation to the assembly of that country in 1949, in which the minister urges opponents of the proposed legislation to consider the fact that "thirty out of the forty-eight states of the United States" have "found it necessary to take legislative steps" of exactly the sort he proposed for South Africa.

9. Sollors, Introduction, *Interracialism*, 6. Sollors cites Heinrich Krieger, *Das Rassenrecht in den Vereinigten Staaten* (Berlin: Junker und Dünnhaupt, 1936).

10. Phillips's most famous utterance on this theme was his address on the Fourth of July, 1863, in Framingham, Massachusetts, in which he endorsed, and called by the name of "amalgamation," that "sublime mingling of the races, which is God's own method of civilizing and elevating the world." The history of the pre–Civil War discourse about amalgamation has recently been clarified by Leslie M. Harris, "From Abolitionist Amalgamators to 'Rulers of the Five Points': The Discourse of Interracial Sex and Reform in Antebellum New York City," in Martha Hodes, ed., *Sex, Love, Race: Crossing Boundaries in North American History* (New York: New York University Press, 1999), 191–212.

11. Sidney Kaplan, "The Miscegenation Issue in the Election of 1864," in Kaplan, *American Studies in Black and White: Selected Essays, 1949–1989* (Amherst: University of Massachusetts Press, 1991), 47–100. Kaplan's classic analysis of the "miscegenation hoax" was first published in 1949. For a recent, authoritative study of the hoax and of the entire discourse about "amalgamation" and "miscegenation" during the antebellum and Civil War eras, see Elise Lemire, *"Miscegenation": Making Race in America* (Philadelphia: University of Pennsylvania Press, 2002), esp. 115–44. Lemire argues that the literary depiction of black-white intimacy helped create the very categories of black and white as these categories had come to be popularly understood in the United States by the time of the Civil War.

12. Even W. E. B. Du Bois used "miscegenation" interchangeably with "amalgamation" and "racial mixing." His learned essay of 1935, "Miscegenation," intended for an encyclopedia but not published during his lifetime, is available in Sollors, *Interracialism*, 461–73.

13. Philip Gleason, "The Melting Pot: Symbol of Fusion or Confusion?" *American Quarterly* 16 (Spring 1964): 20–46. Invocations of the figure of the melting pot in our own time have largely forgotten the

element of anti-Anglo aggression entailed in some of its early formulations. In the climactic scene of Israel Zangwill's play of 1909, *The
Melting-Pot*, a major agent in the popularization of the concept, the Jewish immigrant hero envisages a future in which Mayflower descendants
will be transformed in the fiery crucible and made equal to more recent
immigrants from many lands.

14. Among the few who did this was Zangwill himself, in a fleeting
reference at the very end of his play in one of his lists of the peoples that
"the great Alchemist" would eventually make into one: "Celt and Latin,
Slav and Teuton, Greek and Syrian—black and yellow"; Israel Zangwill, *The Melting-Pot* (New York: Macmillan, 1909), 199.

15. Ralph Waldo Emerson, *Journals and Miscellaneous Notebooks* (Cambridge, Mass.: Belknap Press of Harvard University Press, 1960–82), 11:
299–300.

16. Matthew Frye Jacobson, *Whiteness of a Different Color: European Immigrants and the Alchemy of Race* (Cambridge, Mass.: Harvard University
Press, 1998).

17. Slavery continued in Cuba until 1884 and in Brazil until
1888.

18. For an accessible, pointed discussion of the ambiguities of "In-
dianness," including an account of the popular practice of claiming a
fractional Indian ancestry, almost always through one's grandmother,
see P. S. Deloria and Robert Laurence, "What's an Indian?" *Arkansas
Law Review* 44 (1991), rpt. in Johnson, *Mixed Race*, 312–18.

19. See the tables of the federal census as conveniently available in
Norman R. Yetman, *Majority and Minority: The Dynamics of Race and Ethnicity in American Life*, 6th ed. (Boston: Allyn and Bacon, 1999), 88.

20. Such cases of attempted white-to-black reclassification, while
rare, are not unknown. They are often discussed in relation to minority-
eligible entitlement programs. This phenomenon is addressed in Luther
Wright, Jr., "Who's Black, Who's White, and Who Cares," *Vanderbilt
Law Review* 48 (1995), rpt. in Johnson, *Mixed Race*, 181–83.

21. The standard history of the principle of hypodescent in the
United States is F. James Davis, *Who Is Black?* (University Park: Pennsylvania State University Press, 1991). A readable popular account that increased public awareness is Lawrence Wright, "One Drop of Blood,"
New Yorker (July 25, 1994): 46–55.

22. Barbara Fields, "Ideology and Race in American History," in
Morgan Kousser, et al., *Region, Race, and Reconstruction* (New York: Oxford
University Press, 1982), 149.

23. For the case of the Seminoles, see "Who Is a Seminole, and Who Gets to Decide?" *New York Times* (January 29, 2001): 1.

24. A recent example is the summary discussion by David Parker and Miri Song in the introduction to their edited collection, *Rethinking "Mixed Race"* (London; Sterling, Va.: Pluto Press, 2001), 13–14. A cogent account of the different histories of ethnoracial categorization and related public policies in Brazil, South Africa, and the United States is G. Reginald Daniel, "Multiracial Identity in Global Perspective: The United States, Brazil, and South Africa," in Loretta I. Winters and Herman L. DeBose, eds., *New Faces in a Changing America: Multiracial Identity in the 21st Century* (Thousand Oaks, Calif.: Sage, 2003), 247–86.

25. See the comments on this issue by Christine B. Hickman, "The Devil and the 'One Drop' Rule," *Michigan Law Review* 95 (1997), rpt. in Johnson, *Mixed Race*, 104–10.

26. Alexis de Tocqueville, *Democracy in America*, Harvey C. Mansfield and Delba Winthrop, trans. and ed. (Chicago: University of Chicago Press, 2000), 590.

27. For a detailed account of the legal history of hypodescent prior to its sharpening in the early twentieth century, see Michael A. Elliott, "Telling the Difference: Nineteenth-Century Legal Narratives of Racial Taxonomy," *Law and Social Inquiry* 24 (1999): 611–36. For a similarly detailed account of the history of the U.S. Census's engagement with mixture from 1790 to the present, see Ann Morning, "New Faces, Old Faces: Counting the Multiracial Population Past and Present," in Winters and DeBose, *New Faces*, 41–67.

28. Mark Twain, *Pudd'nhead Wilson* (Hartford, Conn.: Hartford American Publishing Company, 1894).

29. The text of the Virginia "Act to Preserve Racial Integrity" is available in Sollors, *Interracialism*, 23–24. Hypodescent, it should be acknowledged, was not universally applied in all states even after 1924. Louisiana law, for example, was always more responsive to degrees of African descent than the laws of most other states. The inconsistencies of efforts to impose fractional definitions in the laws of various states is a major theme of Teresa Zackondik, "Fixing the Color Line: The Mulatto, Southern Courts, and Racial Identity," *American Quarterly* 53 (September 2001): 420–51.

30. The definitive work on the literary history of black-white mixing is Werner Sollors, *Neither Black nor White yet Both: Thematic Explorations of Interracial Literature* (New York: Oxford University Press, 1997).

31. A discerning study of the sociology of the new "multiracial movement" is Kim Williams, "From Civil Rights to the Multiracial Movement," in Winters and DeBose, *New Faces*, 85–98.

32. For an exceptionally clear and fair-minded analysis of the concept of "race" in the American historical context, see Lawrence Blum, *"I'm Not a Racist, But . . ."* (Ithaca, N.Y.: Cornell University Press, 2002). For a helpful sampling of recent theoretical writings on this concept, see Bernard Boxill, ed., *Race and Racism* (Oxford; New York: Oxford University Press, 2001), especially Boxill's introduction, 1–41, and the opening essay by Naomi Zack, "Race and Philosophic Meaning," 43–82. See also Naomi Zack, ed., *American Mixed Race: The Culture of Microdiversity* (Lanham, Md.: Rowman & Littlefield, 1995).

33. James McBride, *The Color of Water* (New York: Bt Bound, 1999); Shirlee Taylor Haizlip, *The Sweeter the Juice* (New York: Simon & Schuster, 1994); see also Paul Spickard, "The Subject Is Mixed Race: The Boom in Biracial Biography," in Parker and Song, *Rethinking "Mixed Race,"* 76–98. Spickard addresses more than three dozen biographies and memoirs published in the United States in the 1990s. He also engages critically (80–81) one of the most widely read essays of the 1990s on ethnoracial mixture and the one-drop rule, Henry Louis Gates, Jr., "White Like Me," *New Yorker* (June 17, 1996): 66–81, an analysis of the life of "black" writer Anatole Broyard, who passed as white.

34. Philip Roth, *The Human Stain* (New York: Vintage International, 2000). But while Twain allowed the "black" character growing up as white to display disturbing behaviors that played to his reader's suspicions that "black blood" might carry negative propensities, Roth embraced his "black" character in what was, for Roth, the ultimate psychological and cultural solidarity: Roth endowed Coleman Silk with the persona Roth had developed affectionately in novel after novel over the course of thirty-five years, the persona of the neurotic Jewish intellectual. Midway between Twain and Roth, chronologically, another prominent white novelist addressed the theme, but Sinclair Lewis's *Kingsblood Royal* (New York: Random House, 1947) offered white readers few of the concessions Twain did, was covered by none of the conventions of humor that gave Twain great license for dealing with sensitive topics, and was too deeply radical in its critique of racism and of the one-drop rule to generate a positive response from a white readership in the 1940s.

35. The most prominent organizations include the Association of MultiEthnic Americans and Project RACE (Reclassify All Children

Equally); http://www.webcom/intvoice is the web site for another such organization, Interracial Voice. One scholar has counted more than eighty multi-racial organizations established in the United States since 1979; see Williams, "From Civil Rights to the Multiracial Movement," 93. Two volumes of the 1990s that advanced public awareness of this movement were edited by a president of the Association of MultiEthnic Americans: M. M. Root, ed., *Racially Mixed People in America* (Thousand Oaks, Calif.: Sage, 1992); Root, ed., *The Multiracial Experience* (Newbury Park, Calif.: Sage, 1996).

36. For a thorough, scholarly review of the evidence, see Joseph J. Ellis, "Jefferson: Post-DNA," *William and Mary Quarterly*, 3d ser., 57 (2000): 125–38.

37. Woods stimulated extensive public discussion of the one-drop rule in 1997 when he told talk-show host Oprah Winfrey on national television that he was not comfortable being labeled "black," and sometimes thought of himself as a "Cablinasian," a label made up of fragments of "Caucasian," "black," "Indian," and "Asian." For an informative discussion of the controversy surrounding Woods, see Henry Yu, "How Tiger Woods Lost His Stripes," in John Carlos Rowe, ed., *Post-Nationalist American Studies* (Berkeley: University of California Press, 2000), 223–46.

38. The convention of representing non-Anglo ancestry as disproportionately female is often noted in the literature on ethnoracial mixtures. See, for example, Bethany Ruth Berger, "After Pocahontas: Indian Women and the Law, 1830–1934," *American Indian Law Review* 1 (1997), rpt. in Johnson, *Mixed Race*, 71–80.

39. For a memoir of a "black" person who questioned hypodescent only after encountering the *mestizaje* associated with Latinos, see Ranier Spencer, "Race and Mixed-Race: A Personal Tour," in William S. Penn, ed., *As We Are Now: Mixblood Essays on Race and Identity* (Berkeley: University of California Press, 1997), 126–39, esp. 134–35.

40. The law had been modified in 1870 to provide for the naturalization of persons of African descent, but the bar to the naturalization of immigrants from Asia had been mitigated only by the 1943 provision of an annual quota of 105 Chinese immigrants attendant upon the repeal in that year of the Chinese Exclusion Act.

41. Pascoe, "Miscegenation Law," 49, notes that fourteen states had included Asian Americans, under a variety of labels, at one time or another, and that nine did the same with "Maylays," the term long in use for Filipinos.

42. The movement for reparations for Japanese American internees came to climax in 1988 with the passage of the Civil Liberties Act (also known as the Japanese American Redress Bill), which authorized a payment of $20,000 to each victim of internment. Although this figure did not come close to compensating the interned persons for the amount of property loss suffered by many of them, it was an important symbolic gesture.

43. Reynolds Farley, "Racial Issues: Recent Trends in Residential Patterns and Intermarriage," in Neil Smelser and Jeffrey Alexander, eds., *Diversity and Its Discontents* (Princeton, N.J.: Princeton University Press, 1999), 126. See also Roberto Suro, "Mixed Doubles," *American Demographics* (November 1999): 56–62.

44. For a far-ranging discussion of out-marriage by Asian Americans, see Frank Wu, *Yellow: Race in America beyond Black and White* (New York: Basic Books, 2002), 261–300.

45. Gary Nash, "Toward a Recognition of Mestizo America," *Journal of American History* 82 (December 1995): 941–62.

46. Pascoe, "Miscegenation Law," 51–52.

47. For accounts of Perez's suit and of press attention to it, see Mark Robert Brilliant, "Color Lines: Civil Rights Struggles on America's 'Racial Frontier,' 1945–1975" (PhD dissertation, Stanford University, 2002), 129; and Dara Orenstein, "Between the Lines: Mexicans, Miscegenation, and *Perez v. Sharp*," unpublished paper, 2002.

48. *Perez v. Sharp*, 32 Cal. 2d 711, 198 P.2d 17.

49. Neil Foley, *The White Scourge: Mexicans, Blacks, and Poor Whites in Texas Cotton Culture* (Berkeley: University of California Press, 1997), 208, 211. See also Foley, "Becoming Hispanic: Mexican Americans and the Faustian Pact with Whiteness," in Neil Foley, ed., *Reflexiones: New Directions in Mexican American Studies* (Austin: University of Texas Press, 1998), 53–70.

50. For the South Asian and Latino mixture, see Karen Isaksen Leonard, *Making Ethnic Choices: California's Punjabi Mexican Americans* (Philadelphia: Temple University Press, 1992). A helpful discussion of the Supreme Court's 1923 ruling in *U.S. v. Thind* that South Asians were non-white can be found in Ian Haney Lopez, *White by Law: The Legal Construction of Race* (New York: New York University Press, 1996), 86–92. California officials were not always clear whether ethnic Filipinos were covered by the "Mongolian" provision of that state's anti-miscegenation statute. Decisions were made on a county-to-county basis until 1933,

when the state's supreme court, responding to a suit brought by a Filipino American protesting the refusal of the Los Angeles County clerk's office to issue him a marriage license to marry a white woman, ruled that Filipinos were not covered. The legislature promptly added "Malay" to the statute. For California and Filipino Americans, see Leti Volpp, "American Mestizo: Filipinos and Anti-Miscegenation Laws in California," *University of California Davis Law Review* 33 (2000), rpt. in Johnson, *Mixed Race*, 86–93.

51. A convenient listing of the Census Bureau's shifting categories from decade to decade is provided as an appendix to Melissa Nobles, *Shades of Citizenship: Race and the Census in Modern Politics* (Stanford, Calif.: Stanford University Press, 2000), 187–90. For a probing discussion of the role of "blackness" within Latino political solidarities, see Silvio Torres-Saillant, "Problematic Paradigms: Racial Diversity and Corporate Identity in the Latino Community," in Marcelo M. Suarez-Orozco and Mariela M. Paez, eds., *Latinos Remaking America* (Berkeley: University of California Press, 2002), 435–55.

52. For a new study of the politics of the immigration restriction legislation of 1924, see M. M. Ngai, "The Architecture of Race in American Immigration Law," *Journal of American History* 86 (1999): 67–92.

53. For an exceptionally clear and well-informed discussion of the census categories and their relation to ethnoracial mixture, including a review of the specific issue of how to deal with Latinos, see Joel Perlmann, *Reflecting the Changing Face of America: Multiracials, Racial Classification, and American Intermarriage* (Annandale-on-Hudson, N.Y., 1997).

54. For an up-to-date, critical overview of the scientific utility of the concept of "race," see Joseph L. Graves, Jr., *The Emperor's New Clothes: Biological Theories of Race at the Millennium* (New Brunswick, N.J.: Rutgers University Press, 2001). See also the pointed interventions of James F. Crow and Ernest Mayr in *Daedalus* (Winter 2002): 81–88 and 89–94, and by Bruce Wallace in the Spring 2002 issue (144–46) of the same journal. Although the characterization of race as a "social construction" rather than a biological reality has been a mantra in recent decades for people who defend the continued use of "race," a difficulty is that the term long maintained its currency in the English language as a way of denoting exactly those features of a human being that cannot be changed by social conditions, as in the saying, "The leopard cannot change its spots" (which derives from an ancient commentary on skin color, Jeremiah 13: 23, which reads: "Can the Ethiopian change his skin or the

Leopard his spots?"). Hence a term with an imposing history of denoting a permanent, physically embedded, "natural kind" is asked now to refer to contingent social relationships that many advocates of the word's continued use believe can and should be changed. In this context, some discussants (for example, Blum, *"I'm Not a Racist,"* esp. 147–63) now refer to "racialized groups" instead of "races."

55. Farley, "Racial Issues," 126; Suro, "Mixed Doubles," 58.

56. Eva Saks, "Representing Miscegenation Law," *Raritan* 8 (Fall 1988): 39–69.

57. John D. Skrentny, *The Minority Rights Revolution* (Cambridge, Mass.: Belknap Press of Harvard University Press, 2002). See also the essays collected in Skrentny, ed., *Color Lines: Affirmative Action, Immigration, and Civil Rights Options for America* (Chicago: University of Chicago Press, 2001).

58. The somewhat different perspective advanced by leaders of African American organizations in different periods is illustrated by the praise black leaders of the late 1940s gave to Sinclair Lewis's *Kingsblood Royal*, a novel that was in fact based on the life of the light-skinned Walter White, president of the National Association for the Advancement of Colored People. Although the novel's devastating critique of anti-black racism and the illogic of the one-drop rule found little white support, Lewis's implication that blackness was a social construct was welcomed by many black Americans, as readers of the *New York Times* were recently reminded by Brent Staples, "When the Bard of 'Main Street' Turned the Kingsblood Family Black," *New York Times* (August 18, 2002): IV, 12. For a sound analysis of the novel and the difficulties white critics of the 1940s had in understanding it, see Jacobson, *Whiteness of a Different Color*, 265–71. Lewis in effect drew Norman Rockwell's family tree with a black face in it.

59. Michael Novak, *The Rise of the Unmeltable Ethnics* (New York: MacMillan, 1972).

60. The most influential intervention to this effect was Herbert Gans, "Symbolic Ethnicity," *Ethnic and Racial Studies* 2 (1979): 1–20.

61. It should be noted that the unique historical and constitutional situation of American Indians was widely recognized by Congress and the federal courts during this period, even while American Indians were commonly incorporated into the educational and entitlement programs described here. The passage in 1978 of the Indian Child Welfare Act is an example of Indian-specific measures developed during the 1970s.

62. Hugh Davis Graham, *Collision Course: The Strange Convergence of Affirmative Action and Immigration Policy in America* (Oxford; New York: Oxford University Press, 2002); John D. Skrentny, "Affirmative Action and New Demographic Realities," *Chronicle of Higher Education* (February 16, 2001).

63. One Republican senator attempting to discredit all of Affirmative Action observed that the wealthiest monarch in the world, the Borneo-based sultan of Brunei, would be in principle eligible for Affirmative Action if he immigrated to the United States. For this incident, and for an analysis of the decision of most Republicans to live with Affirmative Action despite its lack of popularity with voters, see John D. Skrentny, "Republican Efforts to End Affirmative Action: Walking a Fine Line," in Martin A. Levin, et al., *Seeking the Center: Politics and Policymaking at the New Century* (Washington, D.C.: Georgetown University Press, 2001), 132–71. For examples of press coverage of European immigrants (especially from Portugal) who obtained contracts under Affirmative Action programs, see Graham, *Collision Course,* 154–55.

64. Just how far the need to clarify the basis for entitlements for non-blacks was from almost everyone's mind is indicated by the character of the discussion that took place in 1965 at the single hearing held by the Equal Employment Opportunity Commission on EEO-1, the precedent-setting employer reporting form that became the model for later Affirmative Action documents throughout federal and state officialdoms and in the private sector. Although this form was defined by the four classic "minorities" of the ethnoracial pentagon that were made general to the entire federal bureaucracy in 1977 through the legendary Statistical Directive No. 15 of the Office of Management and Budget, no voice at the hearing commented even in passing on the non-black minorities. Everyone assumed the non-black groups to be so tiny a part of the picture as to require no discussion and to entail no policy dilemmas in the future. I owe this information about the EEOC hearing to John D. Skrentny.

65. A prominent example of a vigorous mid-1990s defense of Affirmative Action that avoids the issue of immigrant eligibility is Stephen Steinberg, *Turning Back: The Retreat from Racial Justice in American Thought and Policy* (Boston: Beacon Press, 1995). Steinberg deals extensively with immigration, which he sees as largely damaging to African Americans. But he treats Affirmative Action itself as if it applied only to African Americans, and thus his arguments for its perpetuation, which are grounded in an analysis of the history of that single group, do not speak directly to the specific programs that were being diminished and abolished.

66. This article was completed before the appearance of Peter Kolchin's judicious "Whiteness Studies: The New History of Race in America," *Journal of American History* 89 (June 2002): 154–73. It is possible that more attention to the history of ethnoracial mixture can consolidate the historiographical advances Kolchin summarizes and address more forthrightly some of the desiderata he identifies.

67. Yet the concept of assimilation, long maligned, is now being defended in ways that better enable it to convey part of the story I am calling "amalgamation." See Russell A. Kazel, "Revisiting Assimilation: The Rise, Fall, and Reappraisal of a Concept in American Ethnic History," *American Historical Review* 100 (April 1995): 437–71; Richard Alba, "Assimilation's Quiet Tide," *Public Interest* (Spring 1995); Alejandro Portes and Ruben G. Rumbaut, *Legacies: The Story of the Immigrant Second Generation* (Berkeley: University of California Press, 2001), esp. chap. 3, "Not Everyone Is Chosen: Segmented Assimilation and Its Determinants," 44–69.

68. Out-marriage rates differ considerably within these color-coded descent groups. About 60 percent of persons of Cuban and Puerto Rican ancestry born in the United States marry non-Latino spouses. Persons of Filipino and Korean ancestry born in the United States acquire non-Asian spouses at about the same rate. Mexican and Chinese out-marriage rates are lower. See Jerry Jacobs and Teresa Labov, "Gender Differentials in Intermarriage among Sixteen Race and Ethnic Groups," *Sociological Forum* 17 (December 2002): 621–46.

69. Farley, "Racial Issues," 126.

70. For the 1940 figure, see Arthur Goren, "Jews," *Harvard Encyclopedia of American Ethnic Groups* (Cambridge, Mass.: Belknap Press of Harvard University Press, 1980), 596; for 1990, see Seymour Martin Lipset and Earl Raab, *Jews and the New American Scene* (Cambridge, Mass.: Harvard University Press, 1995), 72. Lipset and Raab rely on the National Jewish Population Study of 1990, which reported that 57 percent of the Jews who had married during the five years previous to 1990 had married non-Jews.

71. Farley, "Racial Issues," 126.

72. That black-white marriages had increased by about 70 percent during the decade of the 1990s was reported by the Census Bureau in its report "Interracial Married Couples," June 29, 2001: in 1990, there were 211,000 black-white married couples, and in 2000 there were 363,000.

73. Randall Kennedy critically discusses disagreements among African Americans concerning mixture-related issues in "Interracial Intimacy," *Atlantic* (December 2002): 103–10.

74. For a defense of the idea that "miscegenation comes close to epitomizing the American experience," in both Latin America and North America, see Earl E. Fitz, "From Blood to Culture: Miscegenation as Metaphor for the Americas," in Monika Kaup and Debra J. Rosenthal, eds., *Mixing Race, Mixing Culture: Inter-American Literary Dialogues* (Austin: University of Texas Press, 2002), 243-72, esp. 244. This hemisphere-centered analysis is also an example of the continued use in some quarters of "miscegenation" as a neutral term.

75. Frederick Jackson Turner, "The Significance of the Frontier in American History" [1893], rpt. in Fulmer Mood, ed., *The Early Writings of Frederick Jackson Turner* (Madison: University of Wisconsin Press, 1938), 183-232. My understanding of the historical significance of the Turner thesis has been influenced by Kerwin L. Klein, *Frontiers of Historical Imagination: Narrating the European Conquest of Native America, 1890-1990* (Berkeley: University of California Press, 1997).

76. Although specialized studies consistent with this view of the history of the United States abound, attempts at synthesis remain rare. One breezy but helpfully provocative effort to outline a national story emphasizing the theme of amalgamation, offered frankly as a "speculation," is in the final chapter of Michael Lind, *The Next American Nation: The New Nationalism and the Fourth American Revolution* (New York: Free Press, 1995), 352-88.

77. I have argued for the centrality of this issue in "How Wide the Circle of the We: American Intellectuals and the Problem of the Ethnos since World War II," *American Historical Review* 98 (April 1993): 317-37; and *Postethnic America: Beyond Multiculturalism*, 2nd ed., expanded (New York: Basic Books, 2000).

78. Herman Melville, *Redburn* (London: Penguin Books, 1986), 240. See also Acts 2: 1-21.

79. *Bulworth*, a film by Warren Beatty, 1998.

Chapter 2. The One Drop Rule and the One Hate Rule

1. For a more extensive account of the historic role of the principle of hypodescent, see my "Amalgamation and Hypodescent: The Question of Ethnoracial Mixture in the History of the United States," *American Historical Review* 108, no. 5 (December 2003): 1363-90, from which several paragraphs in this essay are drawn.

2. John D. Skrentny, *The Minority Rights Revolution* (Cambridge, Mass.: Belknap Press of Harvard University Press, 2002). For a vigorous

critique of this book, see Victoria Hattam, "The 1964 Civil Rights Act: Narrating the Past, Authorizing the Future," *Studies in American Political Development* 18 (Spring 2004): 60–69, followed by a generally convincing response by Skrentny, "Policy Making Is Decision Making: A Response to Hattam," 70–80.

3. For two overviews of the development of "panethnicity," see Jose Itzigsohn, "The Formation of Latino and Latina Panethnic Identities," and Yen Le Espiritu, "Asian American Panethnicity: Contemporary National and Transnational Possibilities," in Nancy Foner and George Fredrickson, eds., *Not Just Black and White: Historical and Contemporary Perspectives on Immigration, Race, and Ethnicity in the United States* (New York: Russell Sage Foundation, 2004), 197–216, 217–34.

4. I owe this information to John D. Skrentny.

5. Ian Haney López, *Racism on Trial: The Chicano Fight for Justice* (Cambridge, Mass.: Belknap Press of Harvard University Press, 2003), 167.

6. See, for example, Grace Kao, "Asian Americans as Model Minorities? A Look at Their Academic Performance," *American Journal of Education* 103 (February 1995): 121–59.

7. Advisory Board to the President's Initiative on Race, *One America in the 21st Century: Forging a New Future* (Washington, D.C.: Government Printing Office, 1998), 37–38.

8. Ibid., 46, 48, 65, 71–72, 75, 81, 128, 131.

9. Ibid., 126.

10. This suggestion about the census is a variation on proposals made during the 1990s by a number of demographers and social scientists. See, for example, Margo Anderson and Stephen E. Feinberg, "Black, White, and Shades of Gray (and Brown and Yellow)," *Change* 8, no. 1 (1995): 15–18, esp. 18. The substitution of the racial categories with more specific demographic categories would provide individuals greater opportunity to declare their cultural identity while also enabling public and private agencies to pursue anti-discrimination remedies on more empirically warranted grounds.

11. Obama, the keynote speaker at the Democratic National Convention in July of 2004, is the son of a black immigrant from Kenya and a white mother from Kansas. His life story and the questions that story raises about black identity and the dynamics of black progress in the United States today are explored in Scott Malcomson, "An Appeal Beyond Race," *New York Times* (August 1, 2004): IV, 5, and William Finnegan, "The Candidate," *The New Yorker* (May 31, 2004): 32–38.

12. Dalton Conley, *Being Black, Living in the Red: Race, Wealth, and Social Policy in America* (Berkeley: University of California Press, 1999).

13. For an exploration of this terrain, see my "Rich, Powerful, and Smart: Jewish Overrepresentation Should Be Explained Instead of Avoided or Mystified," *Jewish Quarterly Review* 94 (Fall 2004): 596–602. The most ambitious and convincing study of Jewish success is Yuri Slezkine, *The Jewish Century* (Princeton, N.J.: Princeton University Press, 2004).

14. For critical suggestions based on an earlier draft, I am indebted to Victoria Hattam, Jennifer Hochschild, Joan Heifetz Hollinger, Ian Haney López, Rachel Moran, Robert Post, Kenneth Prewitt, John Skrentny, Werner Sollors, Eric Sundquist, and Kim Williams. For other assistance I want to thank Jennifer Burns.

Chapter 3. The Historian's Use of the United States and Vice Versa

1. David Potter, "The Historian's Use of Nationalism and Vice Versa," *American Historical Review* 67 (1962): 924.

2. Prasenjit Duara, *Rescuing History from the Nation: Questioning Narratives of Modern China* (Chicago: University of Chicago Press, 1995).

3. Charles S. Maier, "Consigning the Twentieth Century to History: Alternative Narratives for the Modern Era," *American Historical Review* 105 (2000): 807–31.

4. For one discussion of how the history of the United States might figure in a comparative history of national projects in the modern era, see David A. Hollinger, "Authority, Solidarity, and the Political Economy of Solidarity: The Case of the United States," *Diacritics* 29 (1999): 116–27.

5. David Thelen, "Making History and Making the United States," *Journal of American Studies* 32 (1998): 385.

6. Eric Foner, *The Story of American Freedom* (New York: W. W. Norton, 1998).

7. Linda Kerber, *No Constitutional Right to Be Ladies: Women and the Obligations of Citizenship* (New York: Hill and Wang, 1998).

8. Rogers Smith, *Civic Ideals: Conflicting Visions of Citizenship in U.S. History* (New Haven, Conn.: Yale University Press, 1998).

9. Robert L. Middlekauff, *The Glorious Cause: The American Revolution, 1763–1789* (New York: Oxford University Press, 1982); James McPherson,

The Battle Cry of Freedom: The Civil War Era (New York: Oxford University Press, 1998); David Patterson, *Grand Expectations: The United States, 1945–1974* (New York: Oxford University Press, 1997); David M. Kennedy, *Freedom from Fear: The American People in Depression and War, 1929–1945* (New York: Oxford University Press, 1999).

10. Thelen, "Making History," 374, 394–95.

11. Ibid., 374, 395.

12. Ibid., 394–95.

13. Michael Kammen, "Carl Becker Redivivus: Or, Is Everyone Really a Historian?" *History & Theory* 39 (2000): 230–42; Kerwin Lee Klein, "On the Emergence of *Memory* in Historical Discourse," *Representations* 69 (Winter 2000): 127–50.

14. Of several relevant books by Paxton, see esp. Robert O. Paxton and Michael Marus, *Vichy France and the Jews* (New York: Basic Books, 1981).

15. Kennedy, *Freedom from Fear*, cited in n.9 above. David Thelen, "Re-thinking History and the Nation-State: Mexico and the United States," *Journal of American History* 86 (September 1999): 440–41, and id., "The Nation and Beyond: Transnational Perspectives on United States History," *Journal of American History* 86 (December 1999): 974.

16. Kennedy, *Freedom from Fear*, 855–56.

17. Daniel T. Rodgers, *Atlantic Crossings: Social Politics in a Progressive Age* (Cambridge, Mass.: Belknap Press of Harvard University Press, 1998), 508.

18. James T. Kloppenberg, *Uncertain Victory: Social Democracy and Progressivism in European and American Thought, 1870–1920* (New York: Oxford University Press, 1986).

19. Thelen, "Making History," 380.

20. Henry F. May, *The Enlightenment in America* (New York: Oxford University Press, 1976); Bruce Kuklick, *The Rise of American Philosophy* (New Haven, Conn.: Yale University Press, 1977); *Victorian America*, ed. Daniel Walker Howe (Philadelphia: University of Pennsylvania Press, 1976); James R. Moore, *The Post-Darwinian Controversies* (Cambridge; New York: Cambridge University Press, 1979). Prominent examples from the late 1960s include David Brion Davis, *The Problem of Slavery in Western Culture* (Ithaca, N.Y.: Cornell University Press, 1967), and Robert Kelley, *The Transatlantic Persuasion: The Liberal-Democratic Mind in the Age of Gladstone* (New York: Knopf, 1969). In "American Intellectual History: Some Issues for the 1980s," *Reviews in American History* 10 (1982): 306–17,

building on this tradition of scholarship, I sketched an explicit agenda for an internationally oriented approach to the intellectual history of the United States, designed to operate simultaneously with a more nation-centered research agenda.

21. J. T. Merz, *A History of European Thought in the Nineteenth Century,* vol. 1 (London: W. Blackwood and Sons, 1904).

22. I have argued elsewhere for this one-sentence account of the history of the United States; see, e.g., David A. Hollinger, *Postethnic America: Beyond Multiculturalism,* 2nd ed., expanded (New York: Basic Books, 2000), 220–22.

23. I take these two issues of the *Journal of American History* to be among the most important published by it in recent years.

24. Foner, *American Freedom,* 3–12.

Chapter 4. Money and Academic Freedom a Half-Century after McCarthyism

1. "The Powell Memorandum," *Washington Report* 11, no. 23 (October 23, 1972). This document is printed without page numbers. All of my quotations from the document are taken from this published version in *Washington Report,* which is a publication of the National Chamber of Commerce. Powell's memorandum is dated August 23, 1971. I want to acknowledge that I first learned of this document when it was called to my attention by Michael Wald of the Stanford Law School.

2. Joe Queenan, *The Imperial Caddy: The Rise of Dan Quayle and the Decline and Fall of Practically Everything Else* (New York: Hyperion, 1992), 132–33.

3. Eyal Press and Jennifer Washburn, "The Kept University," *Atlantic* (March 2000): 39–54.

4. I am struck with the ruefully expressed concern of Robert M. Rosenzweig, recently retired after a distinguished tenure as president of the American Association of Universities (the organization of leading research universities in the United States), that many universities in the new rush for dollars may not be able to distinguish between what is central to their mission and what is marginal; see Rosenzweig, "What's for Sale These Days in Higher Education?" distributed by the Center for Studies in Higher Education, University of California, Berkeley, 1999.

5. Rebecca S. Lowen, *Creating the Cold War University: The Transformation of Stanford* (Berkeley and Los Angeles: University of California Press, 1997).

6. A refreshing exception, which appeared after this lecture had been revised for publication, is Masao Miyoshi, "Ivory Tower in Escrow," *boundary 2* 27 (Spring 2000): 7–50. Miyoshi, a professor of literature, treats several of the salient issues in the political economy of higher education today differently than I do, but his article is one of the most comprehensive and honest confrontations of the salient issues written by a humanist. It deserves extensive discussion.

7. J. Hillis Miller, "Literary and Cultural Studies in the Transnational University," in John Carlos Rowe, ed., *"Culture" and the Problem of the Disciplines* (New York: Columbia University Press, 1998), 64–65.

8. I refer here to my service (1996–99) on the Berkeley campus's Committee on Budget and Interdepartmental Relations. The Berkeley Budget Committee, as it has been known informally since its creation in 1919, is unusual among American academia's personnel review committees for the extent to which it brings rank-and-file faculty into the routine governance of the university. The committee's nine members, who are appointed by the Academic Senate to rotating terms of three years each, advise the campus's administration not only on promotions and outside appointments but on all personnel actions, including salary raises, at all ranks in all schools and colleges. The committee meets regularly with the campus's senior administrative officers, with whom it generally maintains cordial and collegial working relations. The experience of chairing this committee 1998–99 made me aware of the challenges to American higher education today that I address in this lecture.

9. Terry Eagleton, "In the Gaudy Supermarket," *London Review of Books* 21 (May 13, 1999): 3. "Nothing is more voguish in the guilt-ridden U.S. academia than to point to the bad faith of one's position. It is the nearest a Post-Modernist can come to authenticity."

10. Edward Said, "Identity, Authority, and Freedom: The Potentate and the Traveler," in Louis Menand, ed., *The Future of Academic Freedom* (Chicago: University of Chicago Press, 1996), 215.

11. Ibid., 227.

12. *The Future of Academic Freedom* includes a helpful discussion of Peirce's relevant ideas; see Thomas L. Haskell, "Justifying the Rights of Academic Freedom in the Era of Power/Knowledge," 43–90.

13. The growth of the New Cosmopolitanism as a movement in American academia during the 1990s is an encouraging sign. For an excellent collection of essays representative of the movement, see Pheng Cheah and Bruce Robbins, eds., *Cosmopolitics: Thinking and Feeling beyond the Nation* (Minneapolis: University of Minnesota Press, 1998). This

volume offers a much richer sense of the movement than the more widely noticed book revolving around a manifesto of the philosopher Martha Nussbaum, Joshua Cohen, ed., *For Love of Country: Debating the Limits of Patriotism* (Boston: Beacon Press, 1996). For an overview of this movement, see David A. Hollinger, "Not Universalists, Not Pluralists: The New Cosmopolitans Find Their Own Way," *Constellations* 8 (2001): 236–48.

Chapter 6. The Enlightenment and the Genealogy of Cultural Conflict in the United States

1. See, for example, Ernest Gellner, *Postmodernism, Reason and Religion* (London: Routledge, 1992).

2. John Gray, *Enlightenment's Wake: Politics and Culture at the Close of the Modern Age* (London: Routledge, 1995).

3. Conor Cruise O'Brien, *On the Eve of the Millennium: The Future of Democracy through an Age of Unreason* (New York: Free Press, 1996); Stephen Toulmin, *Cosmopolis: The Hidden Agenda of Modernity* (New York: Free Press, 1990); Alasdair McIntyre, *After Virtue: A Study in Moral Theory* (Notre Dame, Ind.: University of Notre Dame Press, 1981); Gray, *Enlightenment's Wake.*

4. For an example of deep suspicion of the Enlightenment expressed within the context of the multiculturalist debates, see Robin Kelley, *Yo' Mama's Disfunktional! Fighting the Culture Wars in Urban America* (Boston: Beacon Press, 1997).

5. Lionel Trilling, "On the Teaching of Modern Literature," published first in 1961 and later reprinted in Trilling, *Beyond Culture: Essays on Literature and Learning* (New York: Viking, 1965), 3–30.

6. H. Stuart Hughes, *Consciousness and Society: The Reconstruction of European Social Thought, 1890–1930* (New York: Knopf 1958).

7. For an interpretation of the process by which the modern canon was created and maintained, see David A. Hollinger, "The Canon and Its Keepers: Modernism and Mid-Twentieth Century American Intellectuals," in Hollinger, *In the American Province: Studies in the History and Historiography of Ideas* (Bloomington: Indiana University Press, 1985), 74–91.

8. Carl Schorske, *Fin-de-Siècle Vienna: Politics and Culture* (New York: Knopf, 1980).

9. Richard Ellmann and Charles Fiedelson, Jr., *The Modern Tradition: Backgrounds of Modern Literature* (New York: Oxford University Press, 1965).

10. Robert B. Pippin, "Nietzsche and the Origins of the Idea of Modernism," *Inquiry* 26 (1983): 151; Robert B. Pippin, *Modernism as a Philosophical Problem: On the Dissatisfactions of European High Culture* (Cambridge, Mass.: Blackwell, 1991), 4, 20.

11. For an example of the genre, see Steven Best and Douglas Kellner, eds., *Postmodern Theory: Critical Interrogations* (New York: Guilford Press, 1991).

12. Much of this paragraph, and parts of the previous two, are adapted from my "Postscript 1993" in Dorothy Ross, ed., *Modernist Impulses in the Human Sciences 1870–1930* (Baltimore: Johns Hopkins University Press, 1994), 46–53, which updates an essay of 1987, "The Knower and the Artificer," reprinted in the volume edited by Ross.

13. One of the few books on the modernist-postmodernist divide to gasp this is Andreas Huyssen, *After the Great Divide: Modernism, Mass Culture, Postmodernism* (Bloomington: Indiana University Press, 1986), esp. 188–91.

14. Jean-François Lyotard, *The Postmodern Condition: A Report on Knowledge*, trans. Geoff Bennington and Brian Massumi (Minneapolis: University of Minnesota Press, 1984).

15. Richard Rorty, "Postmodern Bourgeois Liberalism," *Journal of Philosophy* 80 (1983): 583–89.

16. Frederic Jameson, "Postmodernism, or the Cultural Logic of Late Capitalism," *New Left Review* 146 (1984): 53–92.

17. The most brilliant of theses virtuoso performances was David Harvey, *The Condition of Postmodernity: An Enquiry into the Origins of Cultural Change* (Cambridge, Mass.: Blackwell, 1989).

18. Theodor Adorno and Max Horkheimer, *Dialectic of Enlightenment*, trans. John Cumming (New York: Herder and Herder, 1972).

19. Gellner, *Postmodernism, Reason and Religion*, 80.

20. Kwame Anthony Appiah, "Cosmopolitan Patriots," *Critical Inquiry* 23 (Spring 1997): 617–39.

21. Ian Hacking, *Representing and Intervening: Introductory Topics in the Philosophy of Science* (New York: Cambridge University Press, 1983).

22. Michael Ignatieff, *Blood and Belonging: Journeys into the New Nationalism* (New York: Farrar, Straus, and Giroux, 1994).

23. Lawrence Birken, *Hitler as Philosophe: Remnants of the Enlightenment in National Socialism* (Westport, Conn.: Praeger, 1995); I allude to Joseph W. Bendersky's review in *The American Historical Review* 101 (Dec. 1996): 1570–71.

24. Goeffrey Galt Harpham, "So . . . What *Is* Enlightenment? An Inquisition into Modernity," *Critical Inquiry* 20 (Spring 1994): 524–56.

Chapter 7. Why Are Jews Preeminent in Science and Scholarship?

1. Thorstein Veblen, "The Intellectual Preeminence of Jews in Modern Europe," most easily available in Max Lerner, ed., *The Viking Portable Veblen* (New York: The Viking Press, 1948), 467–79. The words quoted here are on pages 474 and 477. The essay was first published in *Political Science Quarterly* 29 (1919): 33–43.

2. Seymour Martin Lipset and Everett Carll Ladd, Jr., "Jewish Academics in the United States: Their Achievements, Culture, and Politics," *American Jewish Yearbook* (1971): 89–128.

3. Paul Mendes-Flohr, *Divided Passions: Jewish Intellectuals and the Experience of Modernity* (Detroit: Wayne State University Press, 1991), 23–53.

4. Dan Oren, *Joining the Club: A History of Jews and Yale* (New Haven, Conn.: Yale University Press, 1985), 261–68 and 326.

5. Stephen Steinberg, *The Academic Melting Pot: Catholics and Jews in American Higher Education* (New York: McGraw-Hill, 1974), 101–3 and 121–23.

6. Seymour Martin Lipset and Earl Raab, *Jews and the New American Scene* (Cambridge, Mass.: Harvard University Press, 1995), 26–27.

7. Nathan Glazer, "Social Characteristics of American Jews," in Louis Finkelstein, ed., *The Jews: Their History, Culture, and Religion*, 3rd ed. (New York: Harper, 1960), II, 1724.

8. Shulamit Volkov, "Jews as Scientific 'Mandarins' in Imperial Germany and in the Weimar Republic," *Aleph* 1 (2001): 250–81, esp. 259–60. For Volkov's earlier study, quoting Freud, see her "Social Origins of Success in Science," first published in German in 1987 but reprinted in *Aleph* 1 (2001): 216–45, esp. 222–23.

9. Veblen, "Intellectual Preeminence," 478–79.

10. Milton Gordon, "Marginality and the Jewish Intellectual," in Peter I. Rose, ed., *The Ghetto and Beyond* (New York: Random House, 1964), 487 and 489.

11. I have discussed these features of the American scene in David A. Hollinger, "Jewish Identity, Assimilation and Multiculturalism," in Karen S. Mittelman, ed., *Creating American Jews: Historical Conversations about Identity* (Philadelphia: National Museum of American Jewish History in association with Brandeis University Press, 1998), 52–59.

Chapter 9. Cultural Relativism

1. Melville J. Herskovits, *Cultural Relativism: Perspectives on Cultural Pluralism* (New York: Random House, 1973), 15 (italics in original). This collection of Herskovits's writings on cultural relativism was put together a decade after his death by his widow, Frances Herskovits, and his colleague Donald T. Campbell. In a thoughtful review of this book, a philosopher declared that the book's importance derived in part from the fact that cultural relativism had "almost never" been defended "by coherent argument," and that almost all of its discussants "seemed to assume that someone else had already set it out somewhere." See I. C. Jarvie, "Cultural Relativism Again," *Philosophy of Social Sciences* 5 (1975): 343.

2. Clifford Geertz, "Anti Anti-Relativism," *American Anthropologist* 86 (1984): 263–64.

3. Ibid., 265.

4. Ibid., 275–76.

5. Margaret Mead, *Coming of Age in Samoa: A Psychological Study of Primitive Youth for Western Civilization* (New York: W. Morrow & Company, 1928), 195–248.

6. Melville J. Herskovits, *Man and His Works: The Science of Cultural Anthropology* (New York: Knopf, 1948), 655.

7. Thomas R. Trautmann, *Lewis Henry Morgan and the Invention of Kinship* (Berkeley: University of California Press, 1987), 20, 222.

8. George W. Stocking, Jr., *Race, Culture, and Evolution: Essays in the History of Anthropology* (New York: The Free Press, 1968), 222, 229 (italics in original).

9. Ibid., 231.

10. Bourne's review of Boas appeared in *Columbia Monthly* 9 (1911): 27–28.

11. Robert Lowie, *Are We Civilized?* (New York: Harcourt Brace, 1929), 3, 296.

12. Richard Handler, "Boasian Anthropology and the Critique of American Culture," *American Quarterly* 42 (1990): 253.

13. Ruth Benedict, *Patterns of Culture* (Boston: Houghton Mifflin, 1934), 21–22. Benedict also used this quotation as the book's epigraph. Benedict introduces the concept of the "arc" on 24.

14. Ibid., 172, 249, 271–72; George W. Stocking, Jr., "Ideas and Institutions in American Anthropology: Thoughts toward a History of the

Interwar Years," in *Selected Papers from the American Anthropologist, 1921–1945* (Washington: American Anthropological Association, 1976), 33.

15. Herskovits, *Cultural Relativism*, 9. This remark appears in a chapter first published as an article, "On the Values in Culture," *Scientific Monthly* 54 (June 1942).

16. Ibid., 9–10.

17. Ibid., 93–94. These quotations are from a chapter entitled "Cultural Diversity and World Peace," which the editors explain was written in 1956.

18. Robert Lowie, "Empathy, or 'Seeing from Within,'" in *Culture and History: Essays in Honor of Paul Radin,* ed. Stanley Diamond (New York: Columbia University Press, 1960), 145–46, 152–56. For Herskovits's appreciation of this essay of Lowie's, see James W. Fernandez, "Tolerance in a Repugnant World and Other Dilemmas in the Cultural Relativism of Melville J. Herskovits," *Ethos* 18 (1990): 162.

19. Christopher Norris, *Reclaiming Truth: Contributions to a Critique of Cultural Relativism* (Durham, N.C.: Duke University Press, 1996).

Index